YOU ARE WHAT YOU CHOOSE

YOU ARE WHAT YOU CHOOSE

The Habits of Mind That
REALLY Determine How We Make Decisions

SCOTT DE MARCHI and
JAMES T. HAMILTON

PORTFOLIO

PORTFOLIO
Published by the Penguin Group
Penguin Group (USA) Inc., 375 Hudson Street, New York, New York 10014, U.S.A.
Penguin Group (Canada), 90 Eglinton Avenue East, Suite 700, Toronto,
Ontario, Canada M4P 2Y3 (a division of Pearson Penguin Canada Inc.)
Penguin Books Ltd, 80 Strand, London WC2R 0RL, England
Penguin Ireland, 25 St. Stephen's Green, Dublin 2, Ireland (a division of Penguin Books Ltd)
Penguin Books Australia Ltd, 250 Camberwell Road, Camberwell, Victoria 3124, Australia
(a division of Pearson Australia Group Pty Ltd)
Penguin Books India Pvt Ltd, 11 Community Centre,
Panchsheel Park, New Delhi – 110 017, India
Penguin Group (NZ), 67 Apollo Drive, Rosedale, North Shore 0632,
New Zealand (a division of Pearson New Zealand Ltd)
Penguin Books (South Africa) (Pty) Ltd, 24 Sturdee Avenue,
Rosebank, Johannesburg 2196, South Africa

Penguin Books Ltd, Registered Offices: 80 Strand, London WC2R 0RL, England

First published in 2009 by Portfolio, a member of Penguin Group (USA) Inc.

1   3   5   7   9   10   8   6   4   2

Copyright © Scott de Marchi and James T. Hamilton, 2009
All rights reserved

LIBRARY OF CONGRESS CATALOGING IN PUBLICATION DATA
De Marchi, Scott
You are what you choose : the habits of mind that really determine how we make decisions
/ Scott de Marchi and James T. Hamilton.
p.   cm.
Includes bibliographical references and index.
ISBN 978-1-59184-286-6
1. Consumers' preferences.   2. Consumer satisfaction.   3. Consumer behavior.
I. Hamilton, James T.   II. Title.
HF5415.32.D43 2009
658.8'342—dc22
2009023418

Printed in the United States of America
Set in Janson Text
Designed by Sabrina Bowers

Acknowledgments

We met at a committee meeting at Duke. The topic was
how to encourage more research by professors from different
fields. Walking out of the meeting, we agreed that, instead of
talking about the idea of interdisciplinary research, we'd get
together and actually do it. Our first paper looked at how to
detect when corporate polluters might be underreporting what is
actually coming out of their smokestacks. Writing that paper led
us to detect something else—the very different ways that we each
approach decision making. Thinking about that question led us
to write the book you are reading.

Getting this book published required someone who loves
risks (since we're new authors writing about new theories), enjoys
information, and thinks about the future. That accurately
describes our agent, Melissa Flashman. Melissa became an immediate fan of the TRAITS model and helped bring our ideas to a

wider audience. David Moldawer, our editor, saved us from a multitude of sins: too many caveats, detours into data descriptions, and aimless anecdotes. For paragraphs without the passive voice, please thank him!

Many people gave us helpful feedback on the book proposal, including Donald Lamm and the Center for Advanced Study in the Behavioral Sciences (CASBS) class of 2008. We owe a great debt to mentors who pushed us over the years to do the interdisciplinary work that led to this project, including John Aldrich, Joe Kalt, Michael Munger, Scott Page, Sam Popkin, George Rabinowitz, Ken Shepsle, and Kip Viscusi. Kim Krzywy, Mattia Landoni, Jacob Montgomery, and Katherine Tiedemann provided excellent research assistance. The Center for Comparative Biology of Vulnerable Populations at Duke funded our work on environmental decision making. De Marchi benefited from support from the Program in Advanced Research in the Social Sciences at Duke. The CASBS provided Hamilton the academic equivalent of Nirvana—a year to write, with the chance to interact daily with colleagues who became close friends too. Finally, we would like to thank Jennifer Harrod, Russ Denton, Lyle Scruggs, and Justin Walker for reading early drafts of the book and providing thoughtful advice.

While the differences in how we approach child rearing gave rise in part to this book, we do agree on one thing: Spending time with our families is the best decision we make each day. We thank them for their patience as we've worked on this book.

Contents

YOU ARE WHAT
YOU CHOOSE

Introduction

Imagine you work in the marketing research division of the Acme Corporation, tasked with selling their latest product: dehydrated boulders. Acme has a loyal clientele, but the CEO says it's time to grow the market beyond coyotes and the occasional irate duck. You decide to gather data on potential customers. And, since you want to do a good job, you read a slew of the latest books on identifying the people who are most likely to buy your product.

What you find is very encouraging. With the help of powerful computers, it's possible to mine publicly available data to find out what causes people to buy dehydrated boulders instead of, say, rocket shoes. All you need to do is collect a lot of information about your potential customers—the more the merrier—and this can be done with ease on the Internet. Voting records, a preference for scotch over bourbon, purchasing decisions and how they finance the major ones, and census information on where they live—it's all there for the taking. You hire a few scientists to uncover the hidden numerical patterns lurking in the data and suddenly you have a marketing campaign.

The majority of social scientists treat decision making as a simple phenomenon that's amenable to this sort of approach. They believe that people look at the options that are available and choose the one that provides the greatest amount of pleasure. The only real variables worth considering are what their preferences are in the first place, and the costs. For some things, like money, social scientists assume people like more of it rather than less. For other things, like a dehydrated boulder, they break the product down into a bundle of characteristics—how heavy it is, how quickly it rehydrates, whether it rolls fast enough to crush a roadrunner. The popular conception is that people choose the bundle they prefer based on how much money they have to spend. So perhaps Acme isn't going down the wrong track; if you find out enough about people, you can probably use this information to predict how they'll make new choices by uncovering their preferences in other areas. You also hope that people with the same demographics will have similar preferences due to a shared culture and shared experiences.

We thought this approach to understanding preferences and choice was incomplete. For instance, our research had previously revealed the strange fact that many corporations, despite access to enormous resources, despite staffs of highly paid executives, were incompetent liars when it came to reporting how much they were polluting. With the help of the same analytical technique the IRS uses to catch tax cheats, we discovered patterns in the reports they issued on their environmental impact that exposed some corporations as polluters.

Simply put, we learned to detect which corporate executives were prone to lie about pollution, and which weren't. The thing that nagged at us was that we surely weren't catching everyone, which meant there were at least three different types of highly paid, probably quite skillful corporate executives: the type that lied badly enough for us to catch them, the type that lied well enough to avoid detection, and the type that didn't lie at all despite the many incentives to do so (like their stock price). All of these executives faced almost identical pressures. They were in the same sorts of industries and wanted to make profits, send encouraging signals to Wall Street, and deal with government regulations. Yet when it came to a vital decision, they acted quite differently.

We were sitting in Hamilton's office two years ago mulling over these questions and, like a lot of social scientists, we started to think about how people make decisions. Choice is at the crux of all of social science, and it's a complicated body of research that a large number of very bright people have worked on. To get a handle on our results on polluters, we started thinking about a less abstract version of the puzzle. If someone from the Acme marketing division went out into the wild without any preconceptions and studied how people actually make decisions, what would they see? Would people, even in a homogenous group like that of corporate executives, make decisions the same way, or would there be a range of distinct types of decision makers? And does the same person approach the choice of her next car differently than she does her next vote or her next date?

SEX SELLS

You may remember high school as a mélange of cliques, pheromones, and schoolwork. This is the first stop for our Acme research team—high school, after all, is where many people learn about dating, and, given the amount of attention most of us devote to it, dating probably has a direct relationship to many other types of choices we make, including consumer goods. Online matchmaking services are one obvious example that we'll look at later in this book—but sex is a component in the marketing of a vast number of other products ranging from cars to beer. It also turns out that the Acme team has considerable help here. Social scientists are very interested in the dating patterns of teenagers, though more to understand the transmission of venereal diseases than to understand their purchasing behavior.

Let's take a real high school of nearly one thousand students that was studied by the sociologists Peter Bearman, Jim Moody, and Katherine Stovel. The team measured all of the dating behavior that took place over an eighteen-month period and found that the average number of dating partners per student was just over one. If all students are more or less the same in their approach to dating, then we might expect to see random pairs of people involved with each other and no overall structure to dating.

In this case, taking the average at face value and believing that all high school students make similar dating decisions would be very misleading. A quarter of the students had no romantic relationships at all. And of those who did, another quarter formed pairs where neither person dated anyone else. A similar number were involved in groups of three people—at any point in time, two of them were paired up and one was the odd person out—but none of the three dated anyone outside the small group during the course of the study. And very few were involved with larger groups (which means all those songs about love triangles are on to something).

There was, however, one exception. The biggest group of all was also the strangest, and accounted for over half of the students involved in relationships during the study. A picture helps to explain the dating behavior of this large group:

DATING BEHAVIOR

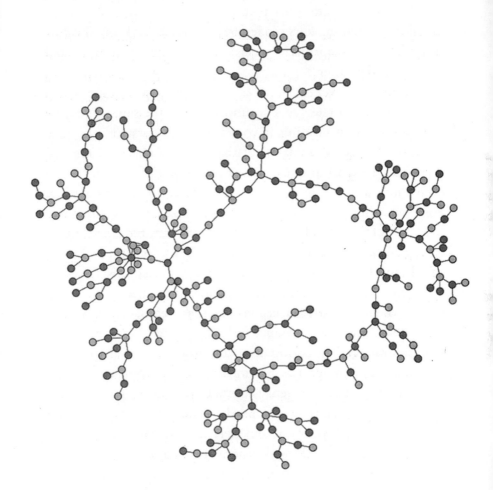

What you're looking at here is a social network; the darker circles are male students and the lighter circles are females. The lines between them represent romantic connections. Some of the students dated more than others (note the male on the left side of the diagram who dated eight females), but all 283 students in this network were connected to each other. To make sense of this group of students, researchers discovered that attractiveness and smoking explained some of the relationships (that is, pretty people tended to date other pretty people, less attractive people did likewise, and smokers tended to date other smokers). In addition, there was a normative decision rule: "Don't date your old partner's old partner."

Taking the average number of partners per student and assuming that all teenagers are more or less the same would be extraordinarily misleading if you want to understand the true dynamics of dating. In fact, relatively few of the students had even one relationship during the time period of the study, and even those who did were embedded in very different contexts. Some were in unconnected groups of two or three, while others were part of the much larger social network pictured above. Once we dig deeper, it's obvious there was more than one type of teenager in this high school, and their choices reflected this diversity.

If you were going to market an online matchmaking service to people who made dating decisions like these teens, or you wanted to create buzz around a product and believed that dating networks also transmit product information, how would you go about forming a marketing campaign? The most important thing to consider would be how very different these teens were from each other. Despite the fact that they were all the same age, went to the same high school in the Midwest, and were (mostly) white and middle class, they were not making decisions the same way.

In fact, these teenagers ranged from lack of interest (or ability) in dating, to being involved in completely exclusive two- or three-person subgroups, to those who are in the huge network shown above. If you thought people made choices in the same way, you'd be wrong. If you thought that demographics or perhaps their preference for a particular brand of beer or car would help explain their preferences, you'd also be wrong. The approach most social scientists rely on in studying human choice doesn't hold up.

PEAS IN A POD

It turns out that the students weren't the only people who were more diverse in their choices than they appeared. After looking at a range of examples where people demonstrated that they were making decisions in very different ways, even though the context and incentives were similar, we discovered that we didn't even understand one another.

Imagine that the Acme marketing department visited us next, with the idea that they'd ask a battery of questions and then talk to us to see what makes us tick. Research using focus groups works this way; the hope is that by studying fewer people, you capture more depth and detail.

Our responses would look nearly identical given the sorts of questions marketers ask. We are within a few years of the same age, and we are both white males. De Marchi has an undergraduate degree in computer science and history from Wake Forest and a Ph.D. in political science from the University of North Carolina; Hamilton has an undergraduate degree in economics and government and a Ph.D. in economics, all from Harvard. There might be enough difference there to excite an academic snob, but not anyone else. Duke even pays us roughly the same amount.

If the marketer collected data on many of our other choices, we'd look even more like peas in a pod. We both are married (with no divorces) and each of us has two boys of almost the same age. We both live in single-family houses filled to the brim with books, and each of us has a Subaru in the driveway (plus we've both owned Volvos in the past). We could go on with this story, but you get the idea: To a marketer, we are clones. To the extent that anyone did research on us, they'd expect us to make similar choices.

POLITICS

We have been friends for some time, and we knew that something was badly wrong with this picture. Even though it looked like we were similar people, it was obvious to us that the way we approached choices was starkly different. And it wasn't that we had different preferences and were acting on them. Instead, it was clear that the process itself, the way we make our decisions, was different.

Our first clue was politics. If you walk into Hamilton's office, you'll see posters and buttons from presidential campaigns neatly arrayed on the walls. If you start talking to him, you'll soon realize that the narrative of his life is intimately tied to politics. His first date with his wife was on the night of Bill Clinton's 1992 convention speech. His oldest son was born on August 17, 1998, the night of Clinton's Monica Lewinsky confessional. And for a Christmas present in 2003, he gave his wife an all-expenses-paid trip to work on the Howard Dean primary campaign in South Carolina. He's a Volvo-driving liberal who teaches Sunday school and helps his community; his eldest son has asked him questions like, "If there are good Republicans, does that mean there are bad Democrats?"

De Marchi doesn't belong to a political party. He's never voted, not even for a class president in grade school. He fantasizes that someday, if he can sneak it past the institutional review board at Duke, he will conduct an experiment to see how much he'd decrease turnout if he handed out "I Voted" stickers freely on the day of an election. Technically, he's in a political science department, but his research is on mathematical models and his friends joke that he's only recently discovered that the United States has a bicameral legislature. Every year, he teaches a class where one of the main lessons is on the irrationality of voting. And every year, at Thanksgiving or Christmas, the subject comes up and his in-laws give him grief for this. It's not that he doesn't think politics is interesting; he just doesn't think voting or becoming a fan of one party is a useful way to spend his time.

ULTIMATE FIGHTING

If politics were the only difference in our preferences, one might pass it off as a flaw in otherwise mirrored images. But it isn't.

Hamilton, like a lot of people who work too much, wishes he had more time to exercise. Whenever he thinks about getting in better shape and has extra time, he attends classes offered at the gym, runs, or lifts weights. He makes time every week to play basketball with his sons. Each member of the Hamilton family is a huge fan of both the men's and women's Duke basketball teams, and it's great fun for the boys to play ball on the same courts as the players they adore. They also paint their faces for games and hand out cookies to the other fans waiting in line.

De Marchi, on the other hand, practices mixed martial arts. If you've ever watched an Ultimate Fighting Championship event, you know that MMA is a combination of boxing, Brazilian jujitsu, judo, Muay Thai, and wrestling. Participants spar until someone is choked unconscious, or taps out because they are about to have a limb broken. The sport attracts a different sort of enthusiast than Duke basketball does—many viewers are in the military or have prior experience in a combat sport—and tattoos are very popular with fighters and fans alike.

De Marchi doesn't watch Duke basketball, and even as an undergrad he didn't go to a single Wake Forest game. The only time he watches a team sport on television is when the Pittsburgh Steelers are playing in the Super Bowl (he's from western Pennsylvania, and that counts for something).

You Are What You Choose

CHILD REARING

Our final example concerns the way Hamilton and de Marchi raise their children. It's not the only difference that could be pointed out, but it's one of the most telling.

Hamilton and his family spent the last year at the Center for Advanced Study in the Behavioral Sciences at Stanford. As part of the fun, they decided to drive to California from North Carolina and enjoy the attractions along the way. The highlight of the trip was a visit to the Grand Canyon. Hamilton, anxious about the depth of the canyon, bought his kids a book on safety at the gift shop. Strangely, they both read it. Once at Stanford, both children were to spend the summer learning Japanese. Hamilton, who has done research on the impact of television violence on children, tightly monitors what his children are allowed to watch. But to provide them with an incentive with their language training, he promised them that if they were successful in reaching certain milestones in learning Japanese, they would get a Nintendo Wii (and finally get to play video games like the rest of their friends).

De Marchi's oldest child, on the other hand, spent the summer wandering the streets of Greensboro, North Carolina. His wife is a partner in a law firm there, and they decided that kids don't have enough time to explore the world and develop a sense of independence. To remedy this, they sent their ten-year-old into Greensboro with ten dollars in his pocket twice each week while school was out. Like the Hamilton kids, he was also learning Japanese, but he had to meet his tutor at the public library after lunch. On most days his mother met him at a restaurant and they ate lunch together. But before and after his lunch date and his language lesson, he was free to do as he pleased. He was a boy of the streets, and discovered diverse entertainments ranging from watching police officers on Segways to visiting antique shops.

I'LL HAVE THE USUAL

If you detect a pattern to the choices made by Hamilton and those made by de Marchi, you're not alone. We set out to study why we were making such different choices, even though we had so much in common. This book is the result of our investigation into the patterns that underlie human decision making. To test our ideas, we started with a large sample, the roughly thirty thousand people who have taken a series of surveys from the survey research firm Knowledge Networks. We also brought in information pulled from millions of buying decisions made on Amazon.com and searches conducted via Google. The results will help you understand your choices and those of your family members. And, intriguingly, they will even help you predict the decisions of people you don't know yet, but would like to: potential customers. You're going to sell a lot of dehydrated boulders.

1

How You Decide

We know a lot about Felix and Oscar. Both agreed to participate in the Knowledge Networks (KN) survey. Both are white, college-educated men with incomes near $85,000 a year. Both are single. The names are pseudonyms—we created them to protect their anonymity—but Felix's and Oscar's responses to the KN survey are real.

We're interested in how Felix and Oscar make choices. Because they are so similar in terms of their demographics, education, and income, few would be surprised to learn that they both like camping, red wine, and photography. Yet many more of their choices differ than not. Felix cares whether a restaurant offers healthy menu options. Oscar, on the other hand, does not.

Felix gets a flu shot, and Oscar doesn't. Felix is a cautious investor; Oscar isn't.

Both men say they considered safety when choosing cars. If
you look closely, though, there is a big difference in what they
are driving. Felix has an Audi A4, rated as a "Top Safety Pick" by
the Insurance Institute for Highway Safety, while Oscar's used
Dodge Ram merited a mediocre score.

How can we account for these differences? The usual explanation is that the differences between Felix and Oscar depend
in part on their backgrounds. This is surely true, but if we use
demographic and socioeconomic factors like age, gender, race,
education, and income to illuminate how people's backgrounds
differ, the case of Felix and Oscar demonstrates that we would
sometimes be misled. These background characteristics make
for good stories, but they are not always useful when we want to
understand how people make choices.

At this point you might ask: If their backgrounds don't help
us to understand Felix's and Oscar's choices, what will? That is
the question we will answer in this book. It may seem to be a
straightforward issue, but not if you approach it as a trained economist would. And if economics as a discipline studies anything,
it's choice.

An economist would tell you that Felix and Oscar have utility
functions. Utility is a measure of how much people prefer things
such as Audi cars or chicken sandwiches. We cannot truly know
what Felix and Oscar like; this is a black box. We can, however,
assume that Felix and Oscar attempt to "maximize their utility,"
or get the most of what they want with the resources they have,
when faced with different choices. By observing the outcomes of
their choices, we can reconstruct their preferences. Either way, traditional economics argues that Felix and Oscar are rational, and we
can assume that they know their own preferences better than we do.

This approach is called rational choice theory, and it has

been a powerful tool for economists. In addition to explaining the buying habits of individuals and organizations, it has been used to examine other types of choices ranging from addiction (both negative—to cigarettes—and positive—to music) to cheating. Steven Levitt, for example, showed in his book *Freakonomics* how schoolteachers in Chicago actually changed student answers to improve scores on standardized tests. Their salaries, it turns out, depended on their students' showing improvement on the tests. Since there was little enforcement aimed at policing the teachers (usually one worries about the students in these situations), it was relatively easy for some teachers to cheat, thereby increasing their own salaries by helping their students.

The job of researchers, however, is to poke holes in theories, and rational choice theory has its share of critics. They point out that many of the decisions we make don't appear very rational.

Imagine you want to cross a street and think like an economist. You might really want to get to the other side. On the Duke University campus where we both work, there is a great place to buy hot dogs, named Pauly Dogs, and both of us have to cross a street to get there from our offices.

It's safe to assume that we like hot dogs; otherwise, we wouldn't take the time out of our day and the money out of our wallets to buy them. But crossing the street presents a rub—there is some probability that we will be run over and killed by a crazed motorist. At Duke, they'd probably be driving a BMW, but getting hit by a premium brand feels a lot like getting hit by a beater. Economists would express these as competing payoffs, one positive and one negative. Even though the probability of getting a good hot dog is very high (Pauly hasn't let us down yet) and the probability of getting run over is very low, getting hit by a car and dying would dampen the pleasure of even a large number of hot dogs.

Another rub is that on cloudy days, only one of us (de Marchi) is likely walk outside and cross the street to visit Pauly's. Even though the annual odds of a person being struck by lightning in the United States are roughly 1 in 700,000, Hamilton remembers the day when a golfer at a course near campus was struck and killed by a bolt. The availability of that memory causes him to overestimate the chance he'll be struck by lightning, and causes him to stay indoors for lunch. If there's a major food recall for hamburger meat, he'll also skip the hot dog. Pauly's doesn't even sell hamburgers, but in Hamilton's mind, the risks from burgers are representative of the risks of fast food (including Pauly's dogs).

So the answer to the question "Why does the economist cross the road?" is that he might not, if a car is approaching, or if it is cloudy or there's a hamburger recall in effect. If rational choice models were perfectly descriptive, Hamilton would process the risks of lightning bolts and tainted foods correctly and end up eating more often at Pauly's with de Marchi. The biases in human risk perception, however, will often cause him to miss the optimal lunch (of two dogs, with chips and chili). In general, people (even economists like Hamilton) have trouble with all sorts of choices involving small probabilities, high payoffs, and changing their actions based on evidence. This is by no means the only problem one runs into with rational choice theory, nor is this the silliest sort of cognitive mistake we make. Gift giving, for example, is a conundrum for economists. If you give people gifts, you must have the conceit that you know their preferences better than they do; otherwise why not just give cash and let them buy what they really want? Or consider the practice of picking lucky numbers to play the lottery. It's bad enough that people play the lottery (your expected returns are always negative, else the lottery wouldn't make money), but some of them pay money for schemes to play the lottery "better."

There are, however, a minority of economists who are comfortable conducting experiments in a psychology lab and who focus on the irrational side of things. Behavioral economists point out the ways in which people make systematic mistakes in their thinking, and thus fail to act in accordance with rational choice theory. One of the pioneers of this approach, Herbert Simon, famously argued that people were like ants on a beach:

> We watch an ant make his laborious way across a wind- and wave-molded beach. He moves ahead, angles to the right to ease his climb up a steep dunelet, detours around a pebble, stops for a moment to exchange information with a compatriot. Thus he makes his weaving, halting way back to his home. So as not to anthropomorphize about his purposes, I sketch the path on a piece of paper. It is a sequence of irregular, angular segments—not quite a random walk, for it has an underlying sense of direction, of aiming toward a goal.
>
> I show the unlabeled sketch to a friend. Whose path is it? An expert skier, perhaps, slaloming down a steep and somewhat rocky slope. Or a sloop, beating upwind in a channel dotted with islands or shoals. Perhaps it is a path in a more abstract space: the course of search of a student seeking the proof of a theorem in geometry. . . .
>
> Viewed as a geometric figure, the ant's path is irregular, complex, hard to describe. But its complexity is really a complexity in the surface of the beach, not a complexity in the ant.
>
> These speculations suggest a hypothesis, one that could as well have been derived as corollary from our previous discussion of artificial objects:
>
> An ant, viewed as a behaving system, is quite simple. The apparent complexity of its behavior over time is largely a reflection of the complexity of the environment in which it finds itself.
>
> I should like to explore this hypothesis but with the word "man" substituted for "ant."

For the behavioral economists in the irrational or boundedly rational tradition, people are more like Simon's ants than supercomputers. They make decisions according to simple rules, called heuristics, that sometimes lead them astray.

One of the better-known heuristics has been studied extensively by none other than Danny Glover of *Lethal Weapon* fame. In 1999, Glover made headlines because of his complaints about New York City cabbies. Even though he was dressed well and had his daughter with him, he couldn't hail a cab in broad daylight. In fact, they'd drive around him to get to a white passenger. Cabbies were inferring that black males were a greater risk, and they weren't paying attention to nonracial cues like wealth or family status.

Crime in New York City has decreased a great deal since Danny Glover's experience. *Good Morning America*, not usually known for its social science acumen, followed up on the tenth anniversary of Danny Glover's complaint by conducting their own experiment. Using a pair of comparably dressed white and black men, they measured how often New York cabbies picked them up. What they found was that during daylight hours, both men had identical success hailing cabs. But once night fell, the black man had extraordinary difficulty as once again cabbies bypassed him to find white passengers.

This shows that heuristics evolve; they can also be exploited. Dan Ariely's book *Predictably Irrational* shows how marketers sell us things we don't need. For example, when Williams-Sonoma introduced bread machines, they had only one model and it wasn't cheap. It barely sold. To solve this problem, they introduced a new, more expensive model—Ariely explains that since people often consider *relative* utility instead of how much they value something in *absolute* terms, the older model started selling quickly simply because it now appeared to be a bargain even though the price hadn't changed. The more expensive model was cognitive camouflage.

What may not be obvious is that economists, whether they are of the rational or irrational stripe, are more similar than not: They have physics envy. Math is beautiful, and mathematical models have power. Models simplify reality—they would not be useful otherwise—and economists, like physicists, imagine that humans are particles endowed with rules of behavior. One set of economists uses rules derived from rational choice theory and another set relies on equally systematic rules governing irrationality, but the approach of treating humans like particles remains.

The irony, however, is that economists have simplified reality even more than physicists have. Where physics has many different types of elementary particles—strange quarks, charmed quarks, muons, gluons—economists have only one. All humans, rational or not, are treated the same. Economists argue about whether this particle is rational or irrational, but there's little sense that there are different kinds of particles that *choose differently*. We will argue that people approach choice in different enough ways that the bestiary of particles must be expanded—different types of people exist, and their choices are not fully comprehensible unless you know what "particle" they are.

Felix and Oscar demonstrate how important it is to discover the complete bestiary of decision makers. Both of them said they wanted a safe car, but only one of them got what he wanted. An economist who believed in rationality would scratch her head and say that there were probably other aspects of the choice of the A4 versus the Ram that we didn't consider—and that if we had, their choices would look a lot more rational. And that in any case their words are beside the point. Their revealed preferences prove that Felix likes one car and Oscar likes another, and that's all that matters.

An economist who believed in irrationality might point out that people make mistakes—perhaps Oscar incorrectly inferred that a big truck was safe because of its size. He got it wrong this time, but using heuristics of this sort might help him in his next choice. Since everyone uses these mental shortcuts, our job should be to find out what these are. When we look at data, though, it's easy to be misled. If we're looking for a particular heuristic to prove its importance, we'll get statistically significant results even though only a minority of our subjects are using it. Perversely, we'll probably ignore the people making the "rational" choice.

But what if both of these approaches are incomplete? What if Felix tends to end up with what he says he wants, and Oscar often ends up disappointed? What would explain that sort of pattern in their behavior?

Our approach to this problem was systematic. Like nineteenth-century naturalists, we started looking for different species of decision makers. In the pages that follow, we reveal six core traits that determine how people make choices. But these traits didn't come out of the ether. To bring more people than just Felix and Oscar into the conversation, we chronicled the decisions of thirty thousand additional individuals. Our sample was also very diverse—we were fortunate enough to have large numbers of respondents from the main racial and ethnic groups as well as the different geographical regions of the country. This gives us a better sense of the core traits that lie behind decisions about flu shots, investing, fast food, and cars and guards against worries that our results might be tied too closely to any particular type of person. By studying groups of people and discerning patterns in their aggregate behavior, we found that not everything about Felix or Oscar (or anyone else) is unique—much of their decision making follows patterns. Though we humans don't like to admit it, we often make choices in ways that are fairly predictable; the trick is to identify which type of decision maker we are.

GOT CHICKEN?

What did you have for lunch today? If you got a chicken sandwich to go, you're not alone. Americans increasingly rely on restaurant fare, including fast food. Calories consumed outside the home have grown from 18 percent of total calorie intake in the 1970s to 32 percent. Nearly everyone reports eating fast food at least several times a year, and Gallup polls find that more than half of Americans eat it at least once each week. When they do eat out, people consume meals that are higher in total calories and fat. As more attention has focused on obesity and healthy diets, restaurants have responded by trying to offer menus that address these concerns. For some people, like Felix, that means lunch is a chicken sandwich.

Consumer Reports rates chicken sandwiches for its subscribers. A 2004 report evaluated twenty different chicken sandwiches. Each sandwich was evaluated on multiple dimensions, including portion size, price, calories, fat, saturated fat, carbohydrates, sodium, fiber, and taste, revealing a wide variety. Total calories ranged from 360 for Wendy's Ultimate Chicken Grill to 950 for Panera Bread's Tuscan Chicken. In taste tests, the Baja Fresh, Boston Market, and Chipotle sandwiches were rated the best. While no sandwich dominated on all measures, the editors at *Consumer Reports* gave three "Quick Picks" as offering the best combination of price, nutrition, and taste: the Baja Fresh chicken taco; the Quiznos Honey Bourbon Chicken; and the McDonald's Chicken McGrill.

From our perspective, the interesting thing about chicken sandwiches is that not everyone picks the same one. After all, *Consumer Reports* probably got it right—some of the options both taste better and are healthier than the others—yet even after reading the article, we would find that people make different choices. Why?

If we accept either the rational or irrational approach to decision making, we're stuck. People choose what they like, and what they like (albeit with some chance of making a mistake) is a black box. Consider, though, that both the choice and the deciders are more complex than we might think. Some options, for example, aren't captured by the standard *Consumer Reports* chart. Subway allows you to replace bread with wraps endorsed by the

Atkins diet (though the editors felt the wraps were "slightly sweet and doughy"), and for you, the freedom to wrap might be important. Or you might care about how the chickens were raised: Whole Foods will sell you a sandwich where the free-range chicken practically walked itself onto your kaiser roll. But if you dig a little deeper, you will discover that federal regulations allow farmers to call a chicken free-range if it was raised in a building with a door leading to open space. The label is not actually a guarantee that the chicken enjoyed a life of fresh air and sunlight before landing in your sandwich, and for that you might skip the Whole Foods sandwich in protest.

And even though *Consumer Reports* did not measure the carbon footprint of each sandwich, that day may be coming as activists make the link between diet and global warming. People for the Ethical Treatment of Animals plastered billboards with a cartoon of Al Gore eating chicken with the caption, "Too Chicken to Go Vegetarian? Meat is the No. 1 Cause of Global Warming." To further attract attention, PETA had a man in a chicken suit drive a Hummer with a banner linking global warming to meat. It's as if eating wasn't a guilty enough pleasure.

There are thus many roads leading to and from a chicken sandwich, and many factors that could determine which one you end up buying. It could be loyalty ("I've been going to McDonald's since the days of the Hamburglar"). It could be a risk assessment ("If I get the wheat bun that means more fiber; it will lower my risk of colon cancer"). For some it will reflect a high value placed on the future ("Skipping a Quarter Pounder today means less chance of a bypass in the future"). The actions of others may tip the balance ("The South Beach Diet folks are eating the sandwich without a bun"). Altruism can play a role ("No chicken for me—I'm a vegan concerned about global warming"). Even knowing the options that exist cannot be taken for granted ("I enjoy checking chicken stats online and have a subscription to *Consumer Reports*").

It's called fast food, but your decision-making process in ordering a chicken sandwich can be incredibly complex. In the following section, we describe six core habits of mind that affect how you make decisions in all areas of your life. We call these TRAITS: Time, Risk, Altruism, Information, meToo, and Stickiness.

Stop!

Please consider taking the time to determine what kind of decision maker you are by taking the short survey located in the appendix of this book on page 167. The results will be more accurate if you take the quiz now, before reading any further.

CORE TRAITS

Time

Many decisions today have payoffs or penalties that come far in the future. Some people will focus heavily on the pleasure and pain involved with an action today and heavily discount the future. Others will take a longer view and value what happens in the future almost as highly as the present moment. If you have a two-year-old handy (and we do—it's probably underappreciated in the history of science how useful one's own children can be as test subjects), offer the child the alternative of having one cookie now or two cookies in five minutes. They'll choose the single cookie nearly every time. It's only later that children are capable of taking a longer view (based on our kids, somewhere between three and eleven).

. The questions that reveal your discounting index partly concern your health, where actions taken to prevent illness or injury in the future mean costly steps today. When was the last time you saw the dentist? How often do you exercise each week? What is your height and weight (combined to yield your body mass index)? We also look at less vital but still revealing issues such as whether you considered resale value in selecting your car.

Differences in discounting are sometimes visibly apparent. Felix exercises five times a week at a private club. His body mass index is well within the range considered healthy for adults, and he's been to the dentist twice this year. Oscar, of course, takes a different approach, usually passing up the chance to pay a small cost today for a larger benefit tomorrow. He exercises infrequently and has not been to the dentist in more than a year. Not surprisingly, he didn't look at resale value when he bought his truck.

Risk

Risky decisions generally offer some probability of pleasure in return for a chance of pain or loss. Unlike Time, which measures whether you're willing to pay a cost now for gratification in the future, Risk measures how you evaluate dangers and payoffs inherent in many decisions. For example, would you choose a conservative therapy that would leave you partially handicapped, or a radical one that might cure you but might also kill you? We use questions about cars, bars, sports, gambling, and smoking to measure how willingly a person accepts risks in their consumer and lifestyle choices. To appreciate how this trait works, ask yourself what a yellow light means: speed up or slow down?

Several other aspects of cars touch on risk. Did you buy the extended warranty coverage, the service protection plan, or road-side assistance? How many moving violations have you had in the last three years? The lifestyle choices we included cover attitudes about bars, smoking, and perceptions of whether smoking in moderation was bad for you and whether secondhand smoke was as bad as the media coverage implies. From a list of twenty-four risky sports (auto racing to windsurfing), we calculated the number of sports people indicated they had participated in. From a list of ten types of gambling (from poker in casinos to lottery tickets), we considered the number each respondent had tried along with how frequently they gambled.

There is a wide variation in approaches to risk, even between people that are similar in many respects. If you followed Oscar and Felix around, for example, you'd have very different days. Oscar smokes occasionally and drives fast. He likes to take chances off the road too—he gambles at least once a month and says he's played hockey in the last twelve months. Felix has a much lower Risk index. He never smokes, has had no moving violations over the last three years, and focuses on driving while in the car: no cell phone, no eating. He's never been to a casino and doesn't play the lottery. He's also not into extreme sports. While he has played Frisbee and tennis, he has never gone downhill skiing, motorcycling, scuba diving, or bungee jumping.

Altruism

Considering the welfare of others is a decision trait we call Altruism. To measure it, we first considered how strongly people agree with statements about paying a price for doing the right thing in two situations: Is it a citizen's duty to serve on a jury even if it interferes with her private life? And should you report a crime even if it might put you in some jeopardy? We next included questions about participating in organizations that benefit the community, such as charitable or nonpartisan civic organizations. Finally, giving blood or donating money to charity also boost your Altruism score.

It is easy to spot the altruists in the Knowledge Networks data. Felix, for instance, is the type of person you see frequently at community events. If there is a blood drive, he's there donating. A knock on his door will generate a check for a local charity. On garbage day there's a very large recycling bin beside his curb. If you looked closely in his cans and bins, you would see that he buys products with recycled content. While his neighbors would not be surprised to learn that Felix scores high on our Altruism measure, asking who is likely to score low might be tougher for people to determine. Lack of altruism simply translates into a lack of action in many contexts. Oscar, for example, scores low on our measure because of what he does not do. He does not respond to a blood drive, give money to charity, believe that you should put up with the hassle and serve on a jury, or make the effort to recycle.

Information

Some people don't consume much information. They see it as time wasting, confusing, or simply uninteresting. Others actively seek out data as a tool that will help with decision making. While there's a cost associated with gathering information, for some decisions—like investing—it can be worthwhile. Then there are the information geeks. They enjoy acquiring knowledge, and read (be it fiction or nonfiction) for the pleasure of it. When this group makes decisions, they search for all the information they can readily find. In their leisure time, they're consuming ideas in the form of books, blogs, magazines, Web sites, and television programs. Their passion for news and information spans topics and types of decisions.

In order to capture a person's Information score, we tap into questions from many different areas. How many books did you buy and read last year? When you make financial decisions, how many sources of information do you consult? How many computers are in the house, and do you search for news on the Internet? We also included questions about consumer information. One asks whether you enjoy watching advertisements, while the other asks if the number of different brands available in the market confuses you.

Consider Felix again. He's a college graduate and cannot imagine a life without a home computer connected to the Internet. When making financial decisions, he consults all three news sources listed in the survey: magazines, newspapers, and the Internet. Last year he read over forty books, and is an avid fan of multiple cable news networks. Though Oscar is also a college graduate, he doesn't consume as much information as Felix. He doesn't surf the Web very frequently, and when he does make financial decisions, he asks a friend for financial tips. He does like to read, though he can't stand cable news.

meToo

At first glance, many of the goods you buy might appear to involve only a single consumer—you. You're the one wearing the shirt, driving the car, or drinking the beer. Yet one of the factors in choosing a particular brand is how others react to that choice. Many products thus provide two returns to you—the value you gain from using them directly, and the image or identity you convey to others. The degree to which you are influenced by the opinion of others may also involve how many others you're involved with. If you consider your image or your social networks when you make choices, you are other-regarding and score highly on the meToo trait.

This trait is very different from Altruism. Someone who scores high on our Altruism measure cares strongly about the welfare of others and is willing to pay a price to make the lives of others better (which could involve giving blood, serving on a jury, or donating to a local charity). Someone with a high meToo score is focused on others too, but this is because he wants to know what products they are using and how his choices affect his image or friendships. Scoring high on this trait usually means you have extensive social networks and desire frequent contact with a large number of friends and family members. Yet having an extensive network does not imply you're altruistic; there's often a difference between hanging out with your friends (which is the meToo trait) and serving food at the local soup kitchen (which is Altruism).

Some of the meToo questions concern status: whether you prefer brands that make you feel accepted by others or products or services that are used by lots of other people. We also include questions about how much brand image matters to you in choices like your preferred alcoholic beverage and your car. Other questions tap into how connected you are to a community by asking whether you feel in touch with the people around you, enjoy being part of several networks of people who share common interests and do things together, and how well you know your neighbors. Some questions even get relative measures of your social interactions by asking about how many relatives live within an hour's drive of your home, how many neighbors you talk with regularly, and how many friends live within an hour's drive.

In 1990, tennis pro Andre Agassi scored an advertising ace in his television commercial for the Canon EOS Rebel camera that proclaimed, "Image is everything." The slogan prompted criticism from sports analysts, praise from ad execs, and sales among consumers. Oscar may not be able to recall that ad. But his responses show that he shares the sentiment voiced in the commercial. Oscar likes to order what others are having when he's out at a bar, and admits that he buys products that make him feel accepted by others. And there may be a lot of others involved, since he reports having many friends close by and talking frequently with his neighbors. While Oscar scores near the top of our other-regarding measure, Felix's approach to consuming reflects a much lower concern with image and others. Though Felix is nearly the same age as Oscar and they both possess similar incomes, Felix doesn't buy status items and strongly disagrees with the idea that you can distinguish successful people by how they dress or what they own. There is, however, an Audi in Felix's driveway, which means that deep down he might care just a little what others think.

Stickiness

The final trait underlying choice is Stickiness, or loyalty. Some consumers consider many options when they buy a product and rethink their choices frequently. They buy many varieties of products and shop at different stores. For other consumers, every day is *Groundhog Day* (the Bill Murray film about a man doomed to repeat the same day over and over until he gets it right). They stick with the same products and dealers and don't stray far from the familiar.

We measure this trait by looking at how a person approaches consumer decisions in four areas: cars, cuisines, casual dining, and fast food. Most of the questions capture how comfortable people are with making the same choices they have in the past. How many other makes and models did you consider when buying your last automobile? How many different cuisines do you like to eat?

A low score on the loyalty index reflects a life of variety. Felix considered nine other cars before buying his Audi A4 and had no preference between a foreign or domestic make. He's eaten at four different fast-food restaurants in the last month, and over a three-month period he's eaten at five different casual dining locations. He's also open to many cuisines (fourteen out of the thirty listed in the survey), including such relatively underappreciated options as sushi and Thai. Overall, Felix isn't that sentimental, and doesn't derive any pleasure from revisiting old choices.

In contrast, Oscar's choices scored near the top on the loyalty index. He reports that he has a passion for trucks, but only seriously considered a Dodge Ram truck when he made his last purchase. He said that he would only buy American, and that's what he did. He has favorite restaurants and prefers American, Italian, and southwestern cuisine.

These descriptions of Felix's and Oscar's interests in food and cars would obviously be of interest to marketers. If our theory of core TRAITS is correct, however, the loyalty measure we've created not only helps predict their choices across many types of consumer products, but also helps explain their political decisions. We believe that the habits of mind that people use to make decisions are essentially the same across many different types of choices, reflecting what they value and how they reach decisions.

We can summarize the way that Felix and Oscar approach decision making by looking at their overall core TRAITS. Felix is low on Stickiness, Risk, and the meToo trait, while high on Altruism, Information, and Time (i.e., he places a high value on the future). Oscar takes the reverse approach. These combinations of TRAITS lead us to predict (correctly) that Felix will look for the healthy options at restaurants and get the level of car safety he's after. Oscar will decide not to get the flu shot and will pursue an aggressive investment strategy.

THE HORSE RACE

So far, we've presented a set of anecdotes about why core TRAITS matter. But other researchers, from economists to political consultants to marketing gurus, have different stories. They might tell you that the brand of scotch or bourbon you drink helps determine your political party, or that iPod users are more likely to be early adopters than Zune users.

To convince you that our research into TRAITS provides more insight into decision-making than the alternatives, we're going to test how well TRAITS explain choices across a wide range of areas. In this chapter and those that follow, we'll look at everything from what cars people drive to whether they get a flu shot to how tolerant they are of homosexuality.

Our horse race will test three different approaches simultaneously in one omnibus model. The first component in our model of choice will be our core TRAITS model using the six variables outlined above and nothing else. The second approach to decision making will be demographics, which we broadly define as a person's gender, age, race, education, income, number of kids at home, and urban or rural living status. In later chapters, we will add even more to this approach (to keep the race interesting!) by including a large set of consumer choices, which is a popular approach in both consumer and political marketing—this is called microtargeting. The final approach to decision making will be your choice of political party. To the extent that there are red states and blue states, we were curious to see how many of your choices align with the political team you cheer for.

In the rest of this book, whenever you see a choice, look for the results of our horse race. While we do not present the technical details of modeling (these are available on our Web site at youchoosebook.com), we do tell you how well each approach fares. Our format is simple: Our omnibus model is evaluated in terms of its predictive power. To understand this, imagine that for each of the decisions we study, we have to predict how one hundred people will choose. A model that gets everything wrong will be scaled to 0; a model that perfectly predicts the choices of all hundred people will be scaled to 100. Keep in mind, though, that even random guessing isn't always wrong, so when you look at our results, it's more useful to see how much better we do than the easy-to-achieve baseline of 50 out of 100 right. Since we are including all three approaches to decision making together in the omnibus model (TRAITS, demographics + microtargeting, and party), the predictive power tells you how tractable the question is if you have access to all of the data required for each of these three approaches. But we also want to know the relative merits of each approach, taken by itself. To show you that, we break down the overall predictive power into the proportion accounted for by each of the three contenders in our horse race.

TRAITS IN ACTION

As we have seen, TRAITS are like a Myers-Briggs personality test for how people choose. In the following chapters, we will explore the relationship between these TRAITS and many different types of decisions. We will also examine why some people make better choices than others, have an easier time learning from experience, and may act more like investors than consumers when the personal costs of living out their worldview become high.

In the remainder of this chapter, we will take our TRAITS for a test run by asking two questions: Who gets a flu shot? And who likes to gamble for money? It's possible that these questions have little to do with one another. One is a question about personal health and the other is about attitudes toward games of chance (and perhaps addiction). As we will see here and in subsequent chapters, our TRAITS model helps explain seemingly unrelated choices. To a large degree, *how* you choose (i.e., what type of decision maker you are) matters more than *what* you are choosing.

NOBODY SNEEZE!

You hold them, you strip them, and you wash them. Some people would rather be dead than strip in public.
—Henry Siegelson, assistant professor of emergency medicine at Emory University

It's terribly sad if that's the situation, that people would rather die than be seen without their clothes on.
—Judi Ditzler, editor of *Nude and Natural*

The preceding quotes were featured in a 2002 story in the *Seattle Times* about the risks involved with a chemical attack. Imagine, for example, that your office building has possibly been exposed to a dangerous toxin. Government officials in gas masks and fluorescent yellow chemical protection suits order you out of the building. Outside, there's a line of your coworkers, and each one is asked to strip naked, dispose of their clothing, and then get hosed down with water.

Not everyone is going to be happy about complying with this, but it turns out to be the best way to deal with a chemical attack. FEMA, for example, has the following advice on their Web page: "Remove all clothing and other items in contact with the body.

Contaminated clothing normally removed over the head should be cut off to avoid contact with the eyes, nose, and mouth." Optimistically, the FEMA article adds that you should wash yourself off with soap and water, bleach and rinse your glasses, and if you have uncontaminated clothing (possibly in a closed drawer), you should change into it before seeking medical help. For those of us unlucky enough to be caught away from the requisite soap and water, bleach, and closed drawer filled with clothes, emergency responders are likely to order us to follow Siegelson's more succinct advice: "Strip and hose down."

What should be a simple decision (strip or die) is complicated by a number of factors. Most of us are comfortable stripping in a doctor's office, but not in front of a crowd. Most of us are also better able to evaluate risk when it is something familiar, not when it is a low-probability event with consequences we have never experienced (e.g., a chemical attack). And there are varying attitudes toward authority, and government officials in chemical suits in the midst of a terrorist attack are not necessarily the easiest people to approach with questions.

This is by no means the only "simple" decision about risk that ends up being complex, in large part because there is a web of causality surrounding these choices. The cervical cancer vaccine is another example, as is childhood immunization. In both these cases, parents can view the same medical information and come to different conclusions about whether the vaccine is worth the cost, how the shots might affect their children's health and later actions, and whether a state should require a particular vaccine. Since people react very differently to all of the foregoing choices, how well does our TRAITS model do in explaining them? Clearly, we'd like to know more about how people react to risks. Improving public health depends to some degree on our ability to predict what people are going to do in these situations.

The KN survey asks about a similar choice: whether or not

respondents got a flu shot in the last year. As with the other choices we have discussed, there's a great deal of variation in how people approach the flu shot. Despite a public campaign by the Centers for Disease Control and Prevention every year along with a great deal of media attention, many people choose not to get a shot or are even distrustful of the vaccine.

Each year between 5 and 20 percent of the U.S. population will get the flu. The CDC estimates that over two hundred thousand people end up in the hospital with influenza complications, and about thirty-six thousand die each year from this respiratory illness. Public service announcements in print and broadcast remind those at high risk (the elderly, children, people with certain illnesses, and health professionals) to get the flu vaccine. The CDC suggests that anyone interested in lowering his chance of getting the flu should get the vaccine. In a typical year, only about one hundred million people choose to get the flu shot or nasal spray, while the CDC recommendations indicate that more than twice that number should do so.

The reason the CDC invests in an ad campaign is that flu shots are never free. Even if your health plan provides them at no cost, there's still the time away from work or family that it takes to drive to the clinic, wait for the shot, and experience the slight prick of pain. For those highly attuned to germs, there's even the risk trade-off of what you might catch in the waiting room from fellow patients. On the other hand, getting the flu also carries costs: fever and discomfort, time to visit the doctor, copays for drugs and appointments, and lost time at work or with friends. For those without health insurance, the monetary costs of shots and prescriptions weigh even more heavily.

With the costs and risks involved, our KN data reveal that most people avoid the vaccine. Forty-four percent say they've never had a flu shot and 24 percent report that they only get it once in a while. The ever vigilant, who get the shot before every flu season, account for only 26 percent of the respondents. About 6 percent say they only get the shot if the prediction is for a serious outbreak that year.

The decision to get the flu shot has many characteristics related to our core TRAITS: the risk of a bad outcome if you don't get vaccinated; costs paid today for benefits in the future; information required to appreciate the risks and find the clinics. To predict the frequency that a person gets the flu shot, we include our three main candidates for understanding consumer and political decisions: demographics, party identification, and TRAITS. In describing this particular decision we also measure a person's experience with the flu (ranging from getting the flu every year and staying in bed to seldom getting the flu and going to work even if you get it).

Not surprisingly, demographics explain a great deal about who gets the flu shot. Older people are much more likely to report that they get the shot each year. This is the group at greatest risk (90 percent of flu deaths are among the elderly) and most targeted by health professionals for flu shot recommendations. Those with more education are more likely to get the shot too. Those with higher household incomes and with kids at home are less likely to get the shot every year, perhaps because getting the shot bears higher costs (i.e., you'd have to take time away from your high-powered job or find someone to stay with the kids while you go to the doctor).

The TRAITS, however, also explain a great deal about who chooses the vaccine. People who accept risks in other parts of their lives (e.g., engage in smoking, risky sports, gambling) are much more likely to roll the dice and choose not to get a flu shot. Those who consume more information, on the other hand, are more likely to get it. They may be more likely to learn about the severity of the flu or run across announcements for clinics offering the vaccine. People who score higher on the meToo trait also get the shot in larger numbers. As those around them get vaccinated they will be more likely to imitate the behavior of family and friends. Altruists, those who show up at blood drives and join local groups, are also more likely to get the shot. By reducing the likelihood of getting the flu, they're also reducing the chance they would spread the illness to others.

What is more interesting is that for many people, going to the clinic does not necessarily depend on their experience with the flu. If people learned from prior flu seasons about their own susceptibility and the severity of outbreaks in their area, then the more frequent and severe their experience with the disease, the greater the incentive they would have to get the shot. But the effect of their past is relatively weak, which means that experience alone doesn't fully explain why chronic flu sufferers make the choices they do.

It is only by adding our TRAITS to the picture that things become clear: A person needs a set of TRAITS conducive to learning, or prior experience with the flu has a minimal effect. If you have had the flu before *and* are a high consumer of information, you get the shot in later years. If you like to look to the decisions of others for guidance, once you've had the flu you're more likely to imitate those who get the shot (peer pressure can be good). If you like to avoid risk and end up with the flu, you are also more willing to get vaccinated the next time around. In this way the core TRAITS help us understand why some people are able to build on and interpret their experiences.

The following graph shows the results of our first horse race. In terms of what we can explain about the decision to get a flu shot, the graph shows the power of each modeling approach on a 0 to 100 scale. As we have noted, demographics explain a good deal about who gets a flu shot, but TRAITS are the clear winner. Party identification and prior experience are the losers.

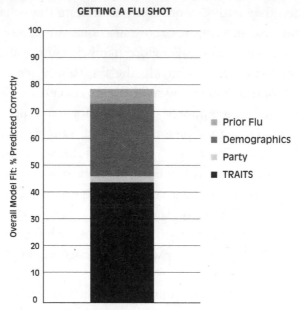

GETTING A FLU SHOT

The bar height shows how many people out of 100 were predicted correctly by our overall model. The shading of the bar shows the relative importance of the different components. For the flu shot, 78 percent were predicted, and the TRAITS mattered most.

TEXAS HOLD-'EM, INTERNET STYLE

Gambling used to be a more intimate enterprise. When the authors of this book were children, there were no personal computers and no Internet. Instead, one of our fathers (of the risk-acceptant author) used to have his hair cut by a barber who doubled as his bookie for bets on National Football League games. Old Italian men would sit and drink Coca-Cola in bottles and talk about the point spreads.

More recently, several books and movies have focused on the activities of some MIT students in the 1990s who took Vegas for millions. These mathematical wizards played blackjack and used their card-counting skills to bolster their odds of winning. Much of the intrigue of the story was fueled by the constant threat of physical violence. If the books and movies are true, there are lots of large, potentially violent men in tacky suits employed by the casinos to take care of big-brained card counters.

All of this, though, is behind the times. If people were going to use their brains to win at gambling today, it would be on the Internet. For the younger set, it's difficult to imagine a time when the Internet was not used for gambling, but it's a relatively recent phenomenon. In ten short years, the business has grown from zero dollars in revenue to over fifteen billion. The question, of course, is who gambles?

Fortunately, we have a wealth of data about gambling habits, and a distinct pattern emerges when it comes to whether or not you enjoy playing games of chance for money. You might think that gambling is a male-dominated enterprise, but that turns out to be false. It is, however, true that churchgoers tend not to gamble (or at least they say they don't) and that Democrats enjoy gambling and approve of casinos at much higher rates than do Republicans. Overall, though, your demographics don't say that much about either your propensity to gamble or your support for legalized casinos in all fifty states.

What does matter, however, are your TRAITS. Risk, obviously, is huge, but there are other highly salient effects. Information lovers love gambling and think that legal gambling should be available everywhere. People with high meToo scores also enjoy gambling in all its forms. And altruists are against gambling, most likely because they're uncomfortable with the addiction that is a component of the activity.

There is an interesting side note: Information lovers do not enjoy playing the lottery. It's obviously not a game of skill, and it's easy to see that the satisfaction people get from playing Texas hold-'em isn't really present in playing the Lotto.

WE HAVE ALL BEEN HERE BEFORE

In choosing a service, product, or a life partner, you face choices between happiness now or in the future, the possibility of a bad outcome, or of your choice somehow affecting others. In deciding what to consume or which cause to support, you can make decisions by gathering a lot of information, looking to others for guidance, or simply deciding to go with what you've always done before. We call our book *You Are What You Choose* because in a sense every choice you make is part of a larger pattern driven by the same core TRAITS.

The connections between getting a flu shot and gambling are not, on the face of it, obvious. We've shown that the decision to get a flu shot revolves around risk, information, and looking to the decisions of others, with a small dose of altruism. It turns out, though, that your attitudes toward addiction, money, and playing games turn on the same underlying TRAITS. If you like information, you like games of chance, and probably prefer to think of them as games of skill. If you enjoy risk, you also get a thrill from taking (and losing) money from friends and bookies. If you're an altruist, you see the darker side of gambling and shy away from it.

In the end, if we're successful, what we learned about what people buy and how they shop should also yield insights into the decisions made by a sample of one: you.

2

You Are What You Choose

In chapter 1, we argued that TRAITS are more effective than the alternatives at explaining how people choose. The problem, though, is that there are a lot of models and a lot of books that all make the same claim. Some of these models treat people as rational, some focus on how irrational everyone is, and some even look at whether you like bourbon or shop at Target and use this information to explain how you make decisions. Both authors of this book worked in management consulting before we became academics, and we can vouch for the fact that there is also a horde of consultants who are happy to claim special (and costly) insight into how people make choices.

If you are the least bit skeptical, you might wonder why you should believe our book.

It's an important question, and one we hope to answer to your satisfaction in this chapter. To make our case, we are going to ask you to think like a gambler. Gamblers understand that there is no such thing as certainty. But it's also true that not every outcome is equally likely. When you make a bet on a football game or a boxing match, you use tools like point spreads and odds to make a prediction. Our approach to testing our TRAITS is not so different. You've already seen, for example, that our TRAITS explain whether or not you are likely to get a flu shot and whether or not you learn from the experience of having the flu. They also explain whether or not you recycle. You might have glanced at our credentials on the dust jacket, and by this point you may tentatively believe we're on to something. But the other authors and consultants have equally impressive credentials, so what would make you put your money, figuratively or literally, on the TRAITS model?

The best way to test a model is to expose it to a wide array of challenges. If we are right and different types of decision makers exist, then we should see the effects of their TRAITS across the spectrum of their choices. This chapter thus has two parts. The first part is about why you should be skeptical of models of any sort, and how you can make better bets when selecting which advice to follow. Think of this first part as an inoculation against bad advice, and as guidance on how to think about our results in the remainder of the book.

The second part of the chapter will try to do something most books don't. We will use our TRAITS to explain a number of very different decisions and see if our approach is better than the alternatives in each case. Are you an aggressive investor? How do you feel about same-sex relationships, and does knowing someone who is gay change your attitudes? Finally, do you drink, and if so, what kind of drink do you prefer?

You will see that TRAITS help explain choices in all of these areas. Our model describes something fundamental about how different types of decision makers operate, and that they don't vary their style of decision making. If they're sticky, for example, and are comforted by the same Egg McMuffin every day for breakfast, we'll show you in this chapter that they probably keep the same portfolio of stocks and tend to be cautious investors.

Once you understand people's TRAITS, you can predict their decisions much better, whether they're investing or deciding whether to invite a gay neighbor to dinner.

FISHY ADVICE FROM WALL STREET

More than half of the winners in the 16th Annual Best on the Street analysts survey are appearing in the rankings for the first time. In a turbulent year for the stock market, these top analysts navigated the markets to find stocks that outperformed, even for part of the year, and others that were best to avoid.
—*Wall Street Journal*, May 18, 2008

He didn't know it yet, but on August 1, 2007, stock analyst Tuna Amobi was about to become famous, at least in finance circles. In nine months, the *Wall Street Journal* was going to choose him as a member of the super-elite group of investors known as the "Best on the Street"—this award would mean huge benefits for him and his firm. Imagine you had a time machine and could go and ask him what his stock picks were before anyone (including him) knew he was one of the best analysts in the country. You might get a leg up on the competition and cash in before anyone knew that Amobi was worth listening to.

Fortunately, we don't need a time machine, because Amobi gave an interview on that day in August and told the world his top three picks. He specialized in broadcasting, entertainment, and discretionary consumer goods, and staked not only his reputation but his clients' money on his picks. It's likely he didn't arrive at his picks randomly, and when asked, he said that even though the areas he studied looked somewhat bleak in the summer of 2007, he was optimistic that you could find winners if you knew how to look for them. Since he was giving interviews on the subject, let's assume he thought he knew how to look.

You can guess where this story is headed. His three picks were Disney, Group 1 Automotive, and Tempur-Pedic. To be fair to Amobi, let's look at the stocks the day he won his award, May 21, 2008, and on August 1, 2008, one year after his stock picks. Both of these dates are before the entire market collapsed. Just for fun, we've also included December 26, 2008.

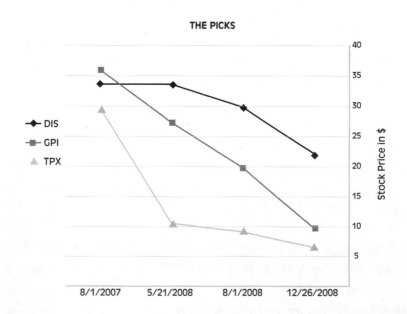

THE PICKS

It's easy to see that Amobi's picks were leading the charge over a cliff rather than following in its wake. In fact, if on August 1, 2007, you had taken Amobi's advice and invested $100,000 split evenly among the three stocks, you would have lost over $29,000 on the day he won his prize, $41,000 a year later, and $44,000 by the holiday season of 2008. This is amazing, because it *underperforms* the S&P 500 by $14,000 and your mattress by $44,000 over the same period.

We're not picking on Tuna Amobi; we're simply trying to make a point (and liked his name). Like most of the winners of the *Wall Street Journal* prize, Amobi will probably not be a repeat winner. In fact, research shows that there's a "winner's curse"—in the year after their awards, the "Best on the Street" do significantly worse than the average analyst. How can this be?

Like us, Amobi studies decision making, albeit in a very particular area: He evaluates how people buy and sell entertainment stocks. Unlike most economists, he must not believe investors are rational. If they were, they'd use the same information he does and evaluate stocks similarly—there's no money to be made from information in an efficient market where prices quickly reflect what is known. Instead, he must believe investors are irrational, and that with his knowledge he can exploit gaps in their heuristics.

Whatever the particulars of Amobi's model of investor decision making, we know that it worked for 2007. But it's possible he just got lucky—after all, someone had to win the investing prize. To distinguish between good luck and a good model, it's important to see how a model performs once you kick the tires a bit by testing it with new data (in this case, the year 2008) or in a new domain (say, financial stocks). This is especially true if you're going to bet money on a model.

"EVERYBODY LIES" (GREGORY HOUSE, M.D.)

As television goes, *House* is not the most uplifting of shows. The main character, diagnostician Dr. Gregory House, is more than a bit of a misanthrope, and his guiding philosophy is that people lie. This applies to patients—House doesn't ask them about their symptoms and histories, because they often hide embarrassing details. Instead, he sends his residents to break into patients' homes to look for evidence of illicit drug habits, spoiled food in refrigerators, or other unsavory behaviors that might factor into illness. It also applies to doctors—House believes that many of his colleagues are fools or frauds.

The problem if you get sick in the real world is that House is not entirely wrong in the latter belief. Doctors have models of how diseases should be treated. When they offer you advice, prescribe drugs, and operate on you, they're making decisions that involve more than your money (though it involves that too). Unfortunately, some doctors are better than others because the models underlying their decisions are better. If you want to find a good doctor or an effective drug, how would you go about it?

According to a number of studies in the past few years, it's not easy. It's been shown that researchers funded by the pharmaceutical industry, for example, are more likely to publish positive results and bury negative results related to these companies' products. Statistical problems are widespread in even the best journals. And at every level, the system of grants, journal editorial policies, and academic rewards inclines researchers to push results out the door—quite possibly a majority of research is falsified within a few years of the publication date because people tend to see patterns where none exist, especially when these patterns help their careers. It's also the case that no one gets excited about research when it finds that the latest miracle drug does *not* cure anyone.

Stock analysts are wrong because their models of decision making are wrong, but doctors are wrong because they often care about finding cures and see results where none exist—it's the reason that medical research uses double-blind trials, in which both the patient and the researcher don't know who gets the actual medicine and who gets the placebo. Just like doctors, social scientists see patterns where none exist, especially since the objects of study (people) are complicated and produce lots of data. At this point, you might ask why models are so often wrong, and how to determine when a model is right.

The answers to these questions are surprisingly simple and can be found by Googling the words "Super Bowl predicts presidential election." You will find that the outcome of the last Redskins home game prior to the election accurately predicts the outcome of the presidency. You'll also see that when an American League baseball team wins the World Series, Republicans do well at the polls, and if an AFC football team wins the Super Bowl, the stock market will decline.

There are so very many of us. In any given year, some of us will produce models of the world that seem to work, and we'll support our claims with data and anecdotes. Imagine four billion hairless apes flipping a fair coin over and over again. A few of them will produce incredible results, like seeing twenty heads in a row, and because these apes are clever (and often self-serving), they'll claim that their expertise or even their psychic powers account for this, not blind luck. Models are often like flipping a coin. They seem to work for a short time, and when they stop working, we invent new models and give new investment or medical or marketing advice.

Look for as many opportunities to test a model as possible. While no one can ever be certain that a model is "true," it does help to keep bouncing it against new problems to see how it holds up. In the sections that follow, we do exactly that with our

TRAITS model. We could still be wrong, and we will point out the limitations of our approach along the way. But with each new area of human decision making we explain with our TRAITS, the odds that we're right increase substantially. And that is the most certainty anyone can offer.

TESTING THE TRAITS MODEL

By testing our TRAITS model in three new areas, we're setting the bar high and hope to convince you that we aren't succeeding by luck. In fact, we're going to make things a lot tougher on our model. In the first chapter, we compared TRAITS to demographics, but it's obvious that even our comprehensive list of demographic characteristics (which included everything from how many kids you have to your socioeconomic status) didn't compete very well. In this chapter, we're going to improve the basic demographics model by adding a large set of behavioral variables. These new variables include whether you rent or own, how often you attend church, the types of alcohol you prefer, whether your kids go to private school, and whether you own a gun.

Microtargeting is the practice of using all of these tiny decisions to predict more interesting things, like how a person votes. An enormous amount of attention, both in consumer marketing research and political consulting, has been devoted to microtargeting. The danger, as we've noted, is that if you give a hairless ape a really, really big data set, he'll see patterns that aren't really there or that don't hold up over time. Our new horse race between the TRAITS and demographics plus microtargeting will allow us to determine the relative merits of both approaches to decision making.

INVESTMENT

*I have a report of a blue BMW speeding, weaving in and out
of traffic, and driving recklessly. Be advised.*
—Heard on a police scanner, as reported by the *New York Times*,
October 17, 2007

To break the land speed record, you need good engineering, but just as important, you need a culture that cultivates people who enjoy risk. Take Britain, for example. Just over a decade ago, a car named the Thrust SSC, driven by a former RAF pilot, broke the sound barrier. A new car, the Bloodhound SSC, looks ready to travel almost 50 percent faster and is propelled by a combination of rockets and Eurofighter Typhoon jet engines.

Americans also enjoy risk, and in addition to the large teams required to challenge the land speed record, they have a related competition for individual enthusiasts who lack the budget to build a rocket sled but still want to go fast: the U.S. Express. This illegal contest is a successor to the Cannonball Run, and involves speeding across the continental United States as fast as possible. Choosing a route and avoiding the police is something of an art form, but the current record holder (allegedly) completed the 2,800-mile journey in thirty-one hours. Alexander Roy drove a modified BMW M5 and had a support team overhead in a Cessna airplane to spot police. Despite publishing a book about the experience, Roy has yet to be arrested and instead has gone on to win the British reality show *The Ultimate Playboy.*

The Finns, in contrast, don't seem to appreciate speed. The only record they hold is on ice, where Juha Kankkunen topped 200 mph in a Bentley. The pool of potential future record breakers—rich, risk-acceptant guys with exotic cars—is depressed because of Finland's unique approach to traffic fines. Risking a speeding ticket there is like high-stakes gambling when the house is rigging the odds, since the fine is proportional to your income.

In 2002, Anssi Vanjoki was caught going 47 mph in a 31 mph zone in Helsinki on his Harley-Davidson, which in the United States would hardly merit police attention. The good news was that as an executive at the Finnish telecom company Nokia, he had the cash to pay the fine. The bad news was that the fine was fourteen days' worth of his annual income, at that point $12.5 million. His ticket came to $103,600, though it was later reduced by 95 percent when he showed the courts that his stock holdings in Nokia had plummeted in value. This reduction took him out of contention for bragging rights on the highest ever speeding fine, which might have made the ticket worthwhile.

And it's not just speed the Finns dislike, it's also gambling. They have a state-controlled monopoly, which the government argues is necessary to keep order. The European Union doesn't see it that way, and has been fighting with Finland to open its borders to online gambling.

Finland's hostility to fast-moving objects and risk in general has helped our research in an unexpected way. Researchers have chosen to study investment behavior in Finland because of the country's comprehensive databases and willingness to share data. Using public records on speeding tickets and stock trades, they showed that those who score higher on sensation seeking, which they measure by the number of speeding tickets a person gets, trade more frequently in the stock market. This is true for men as well as women, which suggests that demographics do not equal financial destiny.

Sensation seeking also includes related behaviors such as gambling and drinking and is very similar to our Risk trait. We don't have the ability to match speeding tickets in the United States to information on how people invest their money, but we can use the Knowledge Networks data to see if our understanding of risk is consistent with the Finnish research. The respondents in the KN survey rated their investment strategies from conservative (don't take risks, prefer lower but expected return), to moderate (balanced risk with return), to aggressive (willing to take high risk for possible return). Most people call their investment strategy moderate and the least likely response is aggressive investing.

What we expect to find is that risk acceptance, whether you're in Finland or the United States, encourages people to invest aggressively. We can also examine which of the other TRAITS affect investing, and whether demographics and microtargeting do as well in explaining what turns a person into an aggressive investor. Compared to our previous contests, however, this one begins with the deck stacked toward demographics. To invest at all (aggressively or not), you have to have money in the first place, so we would expect to see income exerting a huge influence on this behavior. There's also a strong bias toward younger people acting as aggressive investors. Older investors choose less risky investments because they are willing to trade lower average returns for greater certainty that their money will be there to fund their living expenses.

Given these biases, we aren't surprised to find that demographics plus microtargeting are useful predictors of aggressive behavior. And as we expected, age and income are doing almost all of the work. The only other variables that matter are gender and education. Men and the highly educated choose more investment strategies with higher risk.

Yet even after taking into account income and age and net worth, we find that TRAITS explain a great deal about the type of investment strategy a person pursues. People who consume more information choose more aggressive investments. Those who value the future more take higher risks in exchange for later returns. The most influential core trait, understandably, is Risk.

People who show a willingness to accept a small probability of a bad outcome in return for happiness today (achieved through smoking, driving fast, or pursuing dangerous sports) are also more willing to pursue risky investments.

The KN data allow us to investigate one additional aspect of investing behavior. While different people may mean different things by what constitutes "aggressive" investing, one unambiguous fact recorded in our data is how often a person changes their stock portfolio. In this case, the results are much the same as for aggressive investing, with two key exceptions. First, our TRAITS, as a group, matter more than demographics plus microtargeting. To be fair, this is due in part to the fact that people with no stock holdings were not asked the question, thus mitigating the role of age

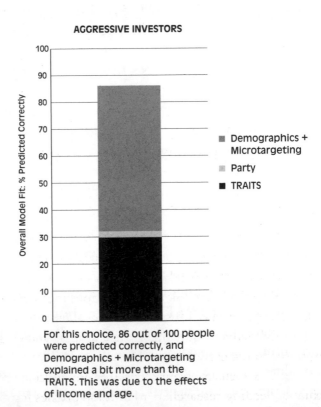

For this choice, 86 out of 100 people were predicted correctly, and Demographics + Microtargeting explained a bit more than the TRAITS. This was due to the effects of income and age.

and income. Second, Stickiness is the dominant trait that explains how people view their stocks. Sticky people buy their stocks and hold them, and knowing where a person lies on our Stickiness scale is much more important than anything else about them.

Taken together, these results on investing are like comfort food. Our TRAITS, while important in both facets of investing, had a split decision with demographics plus microtargeting. It turns out that when it comes to investing, you can be too poor, and not many of us have grandparents who are shorting stocks or buying options. Income and age matter a great deal, and if we had found otherwise, you'd have justifiable cause to treat us as scam artists. What we have shown, however, is that for people who have the time and money to invest, you need to understand their TRAITS to get a complete picture of the strategy they pursue. In this area, a combined model provides the best results.

DRUG CZAR ... CLIMATE CZAR ... GAY MARRIAGE CZAR?

Each election cycle, social conservatives looking for support propose new laws or referenda to prohibit same-sex marriage. The controversy over the issue makes it interesting but difficult to study. Few people would be comfortable giving a stranger information about their sexual orientation or attitude toward homosexuals. Pollsters often ask these questions indirectly or put them at the end of a survey. This camouflages them, and if respondents do get offended and quit the survey, at least you've gotten their responses to the earlier questions.

The U.S. Census essentially punts on questions about homosexuality, leading researchers to develop proxies for determining the number of gay couples in a neighborhood by parsing the data on single men or women living with other single members of the same sex. Private firms will ask for data on sexual orientation, which can be used by marketers to design appeals to gay customers. Yet the way the questions are asked reflects how charged questions about sexuality can be. Knowledge Networks surveys ask people directly for information about many private topics, including health status (e.g., do you have cancer?), child raising (e.g., do you breast-feed?), and medicine (e.g., do you take medication for erectile dysfunction?). When it comes to asking about homosexuality, however, the company adds comforting caveats:

> The next two questions are personal and it is completely understandable if you do not feel comfortable answering them. If this is the case, please indicate that.
>
> 1. Do you have any friends or relatives whom you know to be gay, lesbian, or bisexual?
>
> 2. Are you yourself gay, lesbian, or bisexual?

In addition, KN asks people directly how much they agree or disagree with the following statement: "Sexual relations between two adults of the same sex is always wrong."

Predicting how people answer this question could be as simple as looking at their party identification. After all, gay rights is one of the trifecta of wedge issues that Republicans are credited with using to mobilize their base. Acknowledging this but hoping that it will not always be so, Howard Dean said during the 2004 election, "Sooner or later, voters in places like that [the South] are going to grow tired of voting on guns, God, and gays and start voting on education, health care, and jobs." In the aftermath of the Kerry defeat, explanations of the (many) possible reasons for the loss included calls made in rural Ohio that stressed Kerry's stand on gay issues and the turnout of evangelical Christians primed to vote for ballot initiatives outlawing gay marriage.

But things may not be so simple. Like most ethical or social choices, this issue has both personal and political components. For many people, attitudes toward gays may be based on people they actually know or their own religious beliefs. For others, the political aspects of this issue, such as the Defense of Marriage Act (which prohibited the federal government from recognizing same-sex marriages) and the various state initiatives on same-sex marriage, are important. Perhaps the most famous example of the potential complexity of the issue is the Cheney family, a complexity best illustrated in the 2004 vice presidential debate between Dick Cheney and John Edwards (moderated by Gwen Ifill):

IFILL: I want to read something you said four years ago at this very setting: "Freedom means freedom for everybody." You said it again recently when you were asked about legalizing same-sex unions. And you used your family's experience as a context for your remarks. Can you describe then your administration's support for a constitutional ban on same-sex unions?

CHENEY: Gwen, you're right, four years ago in this debate, the subject came up. And I said then and I believe today that freedom does mean freedom for everybody. People ought to be free to choose any arrangement they want. It's really no one else's business.

That's a separate question from the issue of whether or not government should sanction or approve or give some sort of authorization, if you will, to these relationships. Traditionally, that's been an issue for the states. States have regulated marriage, if you will. That would be my preference. In effect, what's happened is that in recent months, especially in

Massachusetts, but also in California, but in Massachusetts we had the Massachusetts Supreme Court direct the state of— the legislature of Massachusetts to modify their constitution to allow gay marriage. And the fact is that the president felt that it was important to make it clear that that's the wrong way to go, as far as he's concerned.

Now, he sets the policy for this administration, and I support the president.

EDWARDS: . . . Now, as to this question, let me say first that I think the vice president and his wife love their daughter. I think they love her very much. And you can't have anything but respect for the fact that they're willing to talk about the fact that they have a gay daughter, the fact that they embrace her. It's a wonderful thing. And there are millions of parents like that who love their children, who want their children to be happy.

And I believe that marriage is between a man and a woman, and so does John Kerry.

I also believe that there should be partnership benefits for gay and lesbian couples in long-term, committed relationships. But we should not use the Constitution to divide this country. No state for the last 200 years has ever had to recognize another state's marriage.

This is using the Constitution as a political tool, and it's wrong . . .

CHENEY: Well, Gwen, let me simply thank the senator for the kind words he said about my family and our daughter. I appreciate that very much.

IFILL: That's it?

CHENEY: That's it.

Cheney's answer demonstrates that this topic is not an easy party-line choice for everyone—it's an issue of freedom, it's no one else's business, the states should decide, but he supports President Bush despite his reservations. When Edwards brings Cheney's gay daughter into the discussion, an additional and more personal dimension is added to an already complex issue. And for Cheney, that personal dimension produces a flat refusal to discuss the question further.

We thus have two different views of the issue of same-sex marriage. One view is that people use their party identification to answer questions about homosexuality, with Republicans lining up on one side of the issue and Democrats on the other. Our view, however, is very different: We believe people's TRAITS are necessary if we want to understand their preferences on this issue. As always, it may be the case that no model predicts attitudes toward gays; individual opinions on this issue may be just that—too idiosyncratic to account for.

As the graph indicates, decisions about homosexuality are complex, but not random. A fair reading of the results is that everything matters, though not perhaps in the way most of us would have thought. Demographics plus microtargeting once again help explain why people make the choices they do. Personal experience also matters a great deal, which in this case includes whether or not the survey respondent is gay or knows someone who is gay. This makes sense given the Edwards-Cheney debate, which included both factors. In essence, two heterosexual men in traditional marriages displayed a good deal of ambivalence on the issue. Edwards was unwilling to affirm unconditional support for gay marriage (despite his being a Democrat), and one cannot help but think that Cheney's high-minded defense of freedom and states' rights is informed to some degree by the more personal fact that his daughter is gay.

What is hidden by the following graph, however, is one variable that explains much of the success of the demographics plus

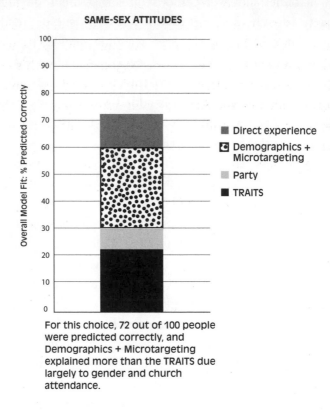

SAME-SEX ATTITUDES

For this choice, 72 out of 100 people were predicted correctly, and Demographics + Microtargeting explained more than the TRAITS due largely to gender and church attendance.

microtargeting approach: church attendance. The good news for our story is that the core TRAITS matter roughly the same amount as demographics and microtargeting absent church attendance; married couples, especially those with children, disapprove of same-sex relationships, as do minorities. This isn't the end of the story, though. Party identification, in relative terms, matters the least of any of the approaches. With all of the media attention that was devoted to the various ballot initiatives on this issue in the 2004 elections, this comes as a shock. People do not neatly line up on this issue based on party identification.

Our analysis reveals additional dynamics about what drives

attitudes that none of the other approaches are capable of. If respondents are gay, this predisposes them to favor same-sex relationships. What is more interesting, however, is when respondents report that they know a gay person. In this case, there is a large positive effect on attitudes toward gays, but this effect is mediated by the Altruism and other-regarding TRAITS. Put simply, if you volunteer and donate to charity and are responsive to other people, the effect of knowing a gay person on your attitude is much greater (roughly 50 percent larger) than it is for less altruistic or empathetic people.

This illustrates the importance of a person's social network and the role of TRAITS in filtering or magnifying experience. If you pay attention to and care about the opinions of other people, then it makes sense for us to look at the people around you if we want to understand how you choose. In the case of the flu shot and same-sex relations, people learn from their experiences based on their TRAITS. If you care about others and worry about their opinions, getting the flu changes your likelihood of getting a shot during the next flu season. Similarly, meeting gays and lesbians raises the likelihood that you end up approving of same-sex relations.

Aside from the learning generated by experience with gay people, the core TRAITS matter in other ways. Information use and risk acceptance both generate higher approval for same-sex relationships. If you're a person who seeks out information or is willing to take risks in life, you're more likely to say that you approve of same-sex relationships. If, on the other hand, you stick with previous product choices, you're less likely to approve of a lifestyle that is only recently becoming more mainstream. As recently as the early 1990s, a majority of Democrats and Republicans did not agree that homosexual relations among consenting adults should be legal, according to Gallup polls.

Overall, our model shows that the TRAITS matter in predicting a person's views about sexual choices just as much as in predicting a person's consumer choices. This is surprising because the questions that make up the TRAITS have nothing to do with social issues, politics, same-sex relationships, or anything similar. Rather, they deal with purchasing habits, what type of restaurants you eat at, or whether you visit the dentist. What does *not* matter as much as expected is your party identification. Journalists often equate views on homosexuality with one's political brand—that is, Republicans condemn gay relationships and Democrats accept or promote them. Our results show that if you're interested in people's views about homosexuality, you're more likely to learn them by asking about their consumer decisions than looking up their party registration.

TO DRINK OR NOT TO DRINK?
THAT IS THE QUESTION

Drinking is more confusing than it needs to be, especially in the United States. We've experimented with Prohibition, and there's a strong belief within many religious traditions that alcohol is sinful. Drunk driving is a continuing tragedy; the number one cause of death for teenagers is automobile accidents, and about a quarter of these accidents involve alcohol. And not everyone gets a fair shake with alcohol. A large body of research has identified genetic factors that increase the risk of alcoholism for some people, and the role of inheritance in alcohol addiction has been demonstrated in both primates and humans.

Despite all this, there's suggestive evidence that in moderation, alcohol is really good for you. The "French paradox" indicates that, to some degree, you can indulge in butter, cheese, and pastries, and as long as you wash it down with a couple of glasses of red wine every day you'll probably live a long, healthy life (at least if you're French). Newer research has identified compounds in red wine, such as resveratrol, that allow obese mice with lousy diets to live nearly as long as calorie-restricted mice. Physicians worry about recommending alcohol, but vintners and wine connoisseurs would argue you should probably drink wine every day unless you have a family history of addiction.

Given this confusion, can our TRAITS help us understand who drinks and even what they drink? It's an interesting problem to study, because there is a never-ending barrage of conflicting stories about alcohol. How do people sort through these messages?

The first thing that's obvious from the data is that both Republicans and Democrats like to drink. The only distinction between the political parties is that Democrats, true to their Volvo-driving, latte-sipping stereotype, prefer microbrews such as Dogfish Head 90 Minute IPA. Demographics and microtargeting produce the expected results. For example, the more educated you are, the more likely you are to drink beer from a microbrewery, probably because you're anxious to show off the fact that you know what an IPA is. If the educated aren't drinking microbrews, then they're drinking wine—along with richer respondents and women. Men overall prefer beer to wine, and churchgoers disproportionately report that they are teetotalers, as we'd expect.

While demographics and microtargeting are useful, they only tell about half of the story. Of our TRAITS, Risk obviously has a role; the more you accept risk, the more you drink. But there are more subtle relationships. Information seekers, for example, prefer red wine, probably because, of all the different types of alcohol, red wine has garnered the most attention for its health benefits. Similarly, respondents who take the long view based on their Time trait, along with altruists, drink less than other people—except, however, for their consumption of red wine. People who are loyal tend to stick to domestic beers and avoid both wine and microbrews. And of all our TRAITS, people with high meToo scores are perhaps the most interesting. By and large, this trait explains only one kind of alcohol consumption, and it's the largest factor by far in explaining it: lite beers. This suggests that if you're drinking a lite beer, it's because you're trying to please others—either you want to lose weight or you aren't acclimated to anything stronger and are drinking to be social.

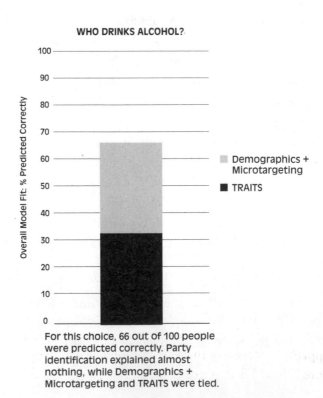

WHO DRINKS ALCOHOL?

Overall Model Fit: % Predicted Correctly

Demographics +
Microtargeting

TRAITS

For this choice, 66 out of 100 people were predicted correctly. Party identification explained almost nothing, while Demographics + Microtargeting and TRAITS were tied.

KEEPING SCORE

Many researchers today focus on how the context and small details involved in a choice are crucial to understanding outcomes. We take a much different view. We believe that a person approaches decisions across different aspects of her life in the same way, and that people differ in these approaches because they have different habits of mind. You make decisions in similar ways because most choices involve time, risk, other people, and information. Choices also build on past choices and at least part of the time have effects on other people.

Why does a particular person have a particular set of core TRAITS? We don't really know, since the TRAITS could arise from some combination of nature, nurture, and culture. In popular discussions, these influences are sometimes captured by demographic factors such as gender, education, and income. Our measures of the core TRAITS do vary somewhat across demographic groups: Men take more risks, women place a greater value on future outcomes, those with more education are more likely to revisit decisions and consider more options when making decisions, and people with higher incomes score higher on our measures of Altruism (e.g., contributing to the community). But by and large, our TRAITS are quite distinct from demographics or microtargeting, and that's why they consistently perform so well in our contests.

If these attributes are so important, why have they gone undiscovered? Economists and psychologists have long studied the separate impact captured by several of our TRAITS (e.g., how people with varying levels of risk acceptance approach smoking, gambling, or the stock market—see references section for more on this). Our work is new because of three insights: People approach decisions in very different ways; people have a set of core TRAITS that are consistent across areas of choice; and, as we'll see in later chapters, our TRAITS help describe consumers as well as fans. The increasing availability of detailed choice data also helped us enormously in formulating this approach.

This chapter shows that the habits of mind measured by our TRAITS help us understand choices that on the surface look unrelated. Across three types of decisions—investments, attitudes toward sexuality, and drinking—TRAITS help predict what you'll buy and what you choose to believe. In the next chapter we'll explore how they can also predict the consequences of your choices and the degree to which you're happy with what you've chosen.

3

Happy, Healthy, and Wise

We cannot investigate what distinguishes good prefer-ences from bad preferences. The fundamental tenet of the social sciences is that people's preferences simply are. It is not, for example, sensible to discuss why someone might prefer chocolate ice cream to vanilla. The simple fact is that some people like chocolate and some like vanilla, and as researchers we have to accept this as a fact if they tell us so. Similarly, some people like to drive green in a Prius and others would rather have the capability to be picked up by a helicopter in their Hummer H1. One cannot argue with preferences.

What can be studied, though, is whether or not people get what they want, learn from experience, and say they are satisfied with their lives. Put another way, are they happy, healthy, and wise? We all know people who are unhappy with their choices; our TRAITS model will help us to understand why some people are more successful than others in satisfying their preferences and improving their capacity to make "good" choices based on their past successes and failures.

One preference that illustrates this point may seem bizarre at first blush. In a recent *New York Times* article, it was reported that almost a dozen times a year people have the urge to fly . . . in a balloon-powered lawn chair. Flight, obviously, has long fascinated humans, but the lawn chair is a relatively modern invention. Obviously, the factors behind such a preference would be difficult for anyone to explain. In fact, it is likely difficult to explain even for those that engage in this pastime. But we can use our TRAITS model to examine how different people come to the decision to take flight in a lawn chair.

The founder of the modern lawn chair flight movement is Lawrence Walters, a.k.a. Lawn Chair Larry. Using only a Sears lawn chair and forty-five helium-filled weather balloons, Larry took flight in the summer of 1982. His plan was to rise one hundred feet into the air, but he misjudged and instead soared sixteen thousand feet into federal airspace (which pleased no one, Larry included). Fortunately, he had a BB gun and used it to land safely, though not without taking down a power line and attracting the attention of the LAPD.

Larry's plan clearly involved the information-seeking attribute—not everyone would have succeeded (albeit with some miscalculation) in putting his flight together. Just as clear, Larry was risk-acceptant and had a very short horizon for his decision making. He was not even sure if shooting the balloons would work; most of his planning concentrated on getting airborne, and he apparently didn't spend an equal amount of effort on a strategy for returning to the earth.

Larry may have been the first, but he is no longer alone. But even within this very select fraternity of lawn chair aviationists, there is considerable variation in how these people attempt to satisfy their preference. Jonathan Trappe, for example, is rated in piloting hot-air balloons. When he flies in his lawn chair, he uses safety equipment and alerts air traffic controllers about his flight plan. While there is still an element of risk acceptance about Trappe's flights, taking off from an airport with a flight plan and an examination of weather conditions indicates that he has high scores for both the meToo and Time TRAITS. He's got a very dangerous hobby, but he cares about other people and the future.

Our last pilot was unfortunately not as lucky as Larry or as well prepared as Trappe. Father Adelir Antonio de Carli of Brazil ascended with the aid of a thousand helium balloons to benefit a local charity, but after he rose to a height of more than nineteen thousand feet, the winds shifted and carried him off course. Despite carrying an assortment of safety equipment with him, he had never learned how to use his GPS unit. After crash-landing at sea, he could not figure out how to turn it on and rescuers were unable to locate him before he drowned. This was not even his first mishap with a lawn-chair-powered flight—six months earlier he was blown off course and ended up in Argentina. His flight instructor had warned him that the winds in the region were dangerous and would "carry him all the way to South Africa."

In this chapter we analyze how TRAITS affect the quality of choices people make. What at first may appear to be random or irrational becomes more understandable when you look at particular patterns of TRAITS. We examine the quality of people's choices in three different ways: Do they get what they say they want? Can they learn from their experiences? Do they end up happy?

BUYING A SAFE CAR

For most of us, a bad trip to Starbucks might mean a spilled latte, a slow barista, or a slightly grating soundtrack. For Britney Spears, it meant becoming the avatar of automotive recklessness in the news. Think about the risk-risk trade-off she faced. While her bodyguard was inside the café getting coffee, feral paparazzi surrounded Spears's SUV as she took her son out of his car seat. When the bodyguard returned, the fearful diva drove off with the child in her lap. Though heavily criticized for not using the car seat, she issued a press release that said, "I instinctively took measures to get my baby and me out of harm's way." Several months later the *New York Post* carried a front-page photo captioned, "Oops, Britney does it again," which showed her child riding in the back of a Mini Cooper convertible in a forward-facing child seat. Car experts observed that the child would have been safer in a rear-facing seat, and according to the *Consumer Reports* Car Blog, "The greater concern should be the apparently loose harness that holds him in place as his body—not just his head—looks slumped over the side of the seat."

Child seat mishaps are just part of Britney's well-chronicled car problems. In a six-month period, she was pulled over for speeding in Beverly Hills, pulled over for driving erratically while trying to avoid the paparazzi, and ran into a Mercedes-Benz while parking in Studio City. In the latter case, she simply left the scene after checking her own vehicle for damage. The owner of the car filed charges three days later after seeing a paparazzi video of the accident posted online. And when Britney left her two young boys alone in the car to dash into a Quiznos restroom, the paparazzi were there again to snap pictures as she emerged. These incidents resulted in a court order forcing her to attend parenting classes and undergo random drug tests.

Celebrities aren't the only ones who find car safety, particularly child seat safety, difficult to understand. Consider Nicole Nason. As a lawyer, she's used to reading fine print, like the kind in a car seat manual. As a former counsel for Metropolitan Life Insurance, she's used to thinking about risk. And as the daughter of a police chief and the sister of an ER doctor, she knows the toll of car accidents. The one time she was pulled over for speeding was by her father, who told her, "If you wind up with a child on your windshield, it will be something you never forget."

When she had a child of her own, Nason let her daughter pick out a pink booster seat with cup holders, like one her friend had. She even attended a three-day class for professionals on how to install car seats. At the class, Nason had what she calls a "eureka moment." She'd gone to the class confident in her abilities: "As a mother of two, I had a lot of attitude going in." Her confidence, though, was shaken when the instructor pointed out that she hadn't been using the right latches to secure the seat in her Honda Pilot.

Nason joined Britney in the news with this story because she was the head of the National Highway Traffic Safety Administration, the government body that regulates child safety seats. Although she'd been the top child seat regulator for sixteen months at the time she took the class, as a parent she'd failed to learn how to install her own seat correctly. She later announced plans for the agency to revisit the "ease of use" ratings for car seats.

The reaction to Nason's admission of ignorance was swift. At Mother Proof, a Web site devoted to the "quest for the quintessential mom mobile," the headline read, "Even NHTSA Boss Can't Get Her Car Seats Right." A staff roundtable revealed disappointment with the regulator's mistake. As one member put it, "I believe her 'eureka moment' should have occurred when she observed there was a latch she wasn't using, because there are just so many useless latches they put on car seats today. You have a eureka moment when you realize you've been wearing the wrong bra size for ten years, not when you're the Boss of the Country's Car Safety and you're not using your car seat properly." A more sympathetic staff member replied that when it comes to car seats, "We're either too proud to admit our errors or we're not educated enough to know that we too have made those mistakes. . . . I'm proud to say that I just had a bra fitting and I was in fact wearing the right size. At least I have control of my boobs, even if I can't figure out how to get my kids' booster seats in the back of a Jaguar XK coupe."

Whether you're a pop star or the head of a government agency, we all make mistakes. But people with high scores on the Information trait tend to cast a wider net when making decisions, and they're more flexible about changing their minds when presented with new facts. We don't usually analyze individual people, but it seems clear that the biggest difference between Spears and Nason is not that they both made a mistake in installing their car seat. The difference is that Nason went to a class on it, learned from her mistake, and ended up getting the car seat installed correctly. To help others benefit from the new information she'd learned in the class, she used her position at NHTSA to help other people get the same information. More generally, though, is it possible to say who is likely to get the safety they say they want, especially for decisions that we care about and make more than once (thereby having a chance to learn from our mistakes)?

To answer this question, we're going to look at a closely related decision. Buying a car can be a confusing process. There's a lot of money at stake and cars have many different features. Of the many things to consider when buying a car, a third of the respondents to the Knowledge Networks survey cited safety as one of the key factors in their choice.

If you ask people to rate the safety of their car, few would probably feel comfortable checking a box that says, "I bought an unsafe car." Not everyone, however, cares equally about this issue; some respondents were much more enthusiastic about the styling or the performance of their cars. For those who did rank safety as their prime concern, we wanted to know if they ended up buying a car that matched their stated preferences. Simply put, did they make a high-quality choice?

To study this question, we combined our KN data with car safety ratings taken from both the National Highway Traffic Safety Administration and the Insurance Institute for Highway Safety. We defined the quality of a decision by looking at the difference between what people said they wanted and what they ultimately drove off the lot. For example, if a person said safety was a very important consideration in the car they bought, did they end up choosing a car that was crashworthy based on the federal and Insurance Institute tests?

As the graph of our results indicates, TRAITS explain a great deal about who gets what they want in car safety. Those willing to court risk in other areas of their lives don't take the time to make sure that their car's safety matches their stated desire. This feature of risk acceptance has a similar effect in many of the decisions we've studied. Whenever we look at the quality of the choices people make, risk-tolerant people make choices that look like they are gambling. They don't appear to devote the time and attention necessary to make sure their choices correspond to what they say they want.

The gap between preferences and outcomes is also greater for those who score higher on Stickiness. If you are loyal to one brand and don't revisit decisions, then you will often face the prospect of choices that don't quite match up. Encouragingly, the fit between desired and actual safety features is closer for those with higher Information scores. If you enjoy acquiring data, there is a payoff: Your choices make you more satisfied.

People with meToo scores that indicate they are other-regarding also get closer to their desired safety levels. This could reflect the status associated with attributes correlated with safety (e.g., my big car is also a safe car), or it could be that friends and families share information about car safety. Finally, those who score higher on Altruism and Time are more likely to get the safety they desire, consistent with buyers who invest the time now to get it right on a decision that will affect their passengers' and their own future.

Surprisingly, only a few demographic characteristics matter. Older people are slightly less likely to get what they aim for. People with higher incomes get a closer fit between the car safety they want and the actual safety provided by their model, but this

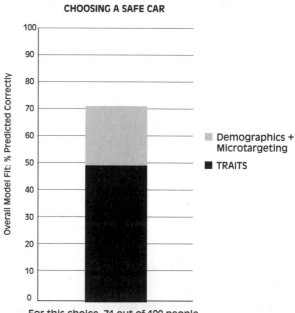

CHOOSING A SAFE CAR

For this choice, 71 out of 100 people were predicted correctly. TRAITS were the dominant component and party identification contributed almost nothing.

is likely an incidental effect of more expensive cars containing more safety features by default.

Though we've focused on the gap between desired safety levels and the actual crashworthiness of the car purchased, the TRAITS also predict other choices dealing with car safety. Depowered airbags are an excellent example. Children or small adults in cars with this safety feature are less likely to be injured by airbag deployment in the event of a low-speed crash, since the airbags deploy with less force.

Overall, the same TRAITS matter in this choice, and again the strongest predictor of who chooses vehicles with this option is risk aversion. People who think more about the future also seek out this safety feature, as do those who score higher on the meToo trait. In comparison, demographics plus microtargeting again matter less than the TRAITS. The only salient characteristics from this model are that women are more likely to get depowered airbags, as are people with higher incomes.

PIMP MY RIDE?

For some people, an ugly car is a safe car, especially if it's an old Volvo. When Dudley Moore played an advertising agent who resolved to make truthful ads in the movie *Crazy People*, he came up with the following slogan: "Be safe, instead of sexy. Volvo." In an essay entitled "The Unbearable Ugliness of Volvos," Stanley Fish noted the affinity of academics for this Swedish import: "One day in the mid-seventies—it may have varied in different parts of the country and at different universities—American academics stopped buying ugly Volkswagens and started buying ugly Volvos, with a few nonconformists opting for ugly Saabs."

Fish notes that the unattractiveness of the car allowed academics to buy a comfortable luxury vehicle without appearing flashy, and that the car's reputation for safety provided a failsafe explanation for the purchase. As he observed:

> Were the car not ugly, a Volvo owner might be in danger of hearing someone say, "My, what a stunning Volvo," to which he or she would have to respond, "Well, perhaps, but I really bought it because it is safe. But no Volvo owner will ever face the challenge of an unwanted compliment.

In 2004, Scarborough Research found that 44 percent of Volvo owners were Democrats and 32 percent were Republicans. This made Volvos the most "Democratic" car brand in America, with Subaru and Hyundai the runners-up. Yet the times are changing, and so is Volvo's appeal. As the company began to stress style and performance in design and advertising, more Republicans bought the car. In a CNW Marketing Research survey of who bought Volvos in 2004, Democrats outnumber Republicans by only 5 percent. As political analyst Mickey Kaus told the *New York Times*:

> Volvos have become more plush and bourgeois, which is a Republican thing to be. . . . Subaru is the new Volvo—that is, it is what Volvos used to be: trusty, rugged, inexpensive, unpretentious, performs well, maybe a bit ugly. You don't buy it because you want to show you have money; you buy it because you have college-professor values.

Knowledge Networks does not ask if you bought an ugly car. The survey does, however, ask if "exterior styling" is one of the reasons you chose your current vehicle over others. The editors at the widely used car rating site Edmunds are willing to take on the fashion challenge and provide ratings for cars' exterior styling—and they're a diverse group of people that includes women, a range of ages, and several minorities. Since we know what car models people in the KN surveys are driving, this means we can compare what they said they wanted in styling to what they actually got (at least in the eyes of the Edmunds editors).

In this decision, our TRAITS matter, but not to the same degree as with car safety. The trait with the greatest impact on the quality of your styling decision is how other-regarding you are, as measured by your meToo score. If you care about appearances in general, you're more likely to get the car appearance you're aiming for. Put another way, the aim of style is impressing other people, and this is a product of caring more about what your social network thinks than anything innate about the car. We also found that people who value future outcomes more are more likely to get an accurate match in car appearances. If they're planners in several areas—for example, making time to exercise, visit the dentist, and buy that auto club membership—they're more likely to make a purchase that gives them what they're after.

When we looked at the quality of car safety decisions, Information and Risk were important factors in predicting whether you got the level of safety desired. Here neither factor has much of an impact. This is probably because less information is required to judge whether a car's exterior is attractive compared to whether it's safe. And though some single people might argue otherwise, the style of your car probably doesn't involve much risk, no matter how ugly it is.

Demographics plus microtargeting did very well in predicting this choice. Men are more likely to get the car fashion they're aiming for. If you have a higher income, you're more likely to get what you want in this as in other markets. If you have kids in tow, you're less likely to get the styling match—perhaps because your spouse is making you drive the minivan.

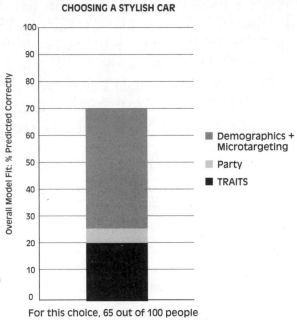

CHOOSING A STYLISH CAR

For this choice, 65 out of 100 people were predicted correctly. Demographics + Microtargeting were the most important component. Of the TRAITS, meTOO mattered the most by far.

APPEAL TO THE RIGHT TRAITS

So far, our work on cars has focused on the consumer side of the equation. But there's a lot to be learned on the marketing side as well. Imagine for a moment that your automobile is differentiated in the market because of its safety record. Alternately, what if you are aiming your product at consumers who consider style first?

Based on our work, it's easy to separate the safety-conscious shoppers from the fashionistas. People who worry about safety will respond to information about crash tests and how likely it is that you will walk away from a head-on collision with a bridge abutment. It goes without saying that you also want to make your potential customers very afraid—in a later chapter, we'll see this in action by looking at a direct appeal on Google AdWords based on making people worry about risk. After all, if they're choosing a car because they are risk-averse, it's worth your time to make them a little fearful of what might happen if they're not ensconced in a safe car. Finally, you might want to let them know that their friends and family will appreciate them for making such a conscientious choice.

On all of these levels, the famous Volvo "Twister" commercial succeeds admirably (search YouTube.com for a look). Sure, not everyone is going to drive their car *toward* a tornado as houses implode and lightning blasts the earth around them, but the protagonist in the commercial is doing it for science. He cares. But he's not stupid: The commercial leaves the strong impression that without the advanced safety technology in his Volvo, he'd be dead meat.

Style is a bit harder to sell, because you can't simply inform the consumer that a car is stylish—almost by definition, that won't work. Instead, our results indicate that you have to create positive buzz in their social networks—the best way to get at the meToo trait is to get a consumer's family and friends talking about your product. There are creative ways to do this, but one of the more common tactics in the last decade has been artificial scarcity. Everything from the Subaru STI to the Mini Cooper was hard to lay hands on at launch. People couldn't buy one immediately, but they were talking about them, and that matters a lot.

The system of TRAITS we've developed is broader than any of these examples, and this is more important than it may seem. Throughout this book, one of our themes is the incredible reach that the TRAITS have; they perform in consistent ways across a range of very different decisions. What we haven't shown you is how poorly the other approach of demographics plus microtargeting does when used alone. On particular decisions, variables such as race or education do well, but they don't hold up across a battery of decisions. And when TRAITS aren't included, their effects are often contrary or absent entirely. We won't take up space to present these negative findings, but the modeling lesson is that if you have the data, it's best to combine TRAITS with more traditional approaches. This is especially true if you want to sell more than one product, or if you're interested in how opinions of your product change over time (as we will see at the end of this chapter).

EATING OUT . . . WITH GUILT

Now fiber is hot, and people are realizing it's more than nature's broom.

> —Keith Ayoob, associate professor of pediatrics at the Albert Einstein College of Medicine, quoted in *Newsweek*, April 16, 2007

Let's switch gears from cars to food, so we can see if wisdom in one area implies wisdom in another. One part of good health is eating well, and if you're the sort that pays attention to such things, you may go out of your way to include a lot of fiber in your diet. Fiber is now important enough to be included on every food label, and store shelves are stocked with a wide variety of high-fiber foods. Some are remarkably pleasant to eat (fruits), and others aren't (to avoid a lawsuit, we won't name names, but some high-fiber breakfast cereals aren't much better than minced cardboard).

For several decades, people thought fiber was especially good at preventing colon cancer. The theory behind this belief was based on the work of Dr. Denis Parsons Burkitt, who worked in Africa in the 1950s and 1960s. He observed that Africans didn't suffer from many of the same diseases as Europeans, particularly colon cancer. Given the location of the cancer and the action of fiber, his hunch was that frequent trips to the bathroom kept your innards clean of pathogens. He actually had two theories to explain the difference, but published a book for a general readership on only one of them: *Don't Forget Fibre in Your Diet*. The other theory, that squatting was a healthier way to eliminate waste, didn't attract as much attention. And thus history was changed.

In 1999, however, everything changed again. The Nurses' Health Study, a data set with tens of thousands of individuals, was used to test the link between fiber and cancer. It found nothing. Since then, advice on fiber continues to oscillate; it's been a busy decade for fiber research. There have been studies on possible health effects of fiber on heart disease, breast cancer, and reevaluations of colon cancer—with mixed results. It's safe to say that at least some fiber, especially that which is found in fruits and vegetables, is good for you.

Obviously, not everyone is paying attention to the intricacies of the fiber literature. And it's not like fiber is the only game in town—there are similar, conflicted stories to be told for drinking lots of water, taking vitamins, and which fats are good or bad for you and in what quantities. We see lots of students lugging huge containers of water (often supplemented with vitamins) to class. Apparently they heard the news from a few years back that lots of water was good for you, but they haven't heard the more recent findings that this advice had been called into question.

As a result, we can't directly measure whether or not someone is eating a healthy diet. All we can look at is whether or not someone says they're trying to eat a healthy diet. One facet of the daily struggle to eat healthy food is where you eat out. The variety in restaurants is enormous, and people have no difficulty finding healthy options if they want them. But clearly, not everyone does. Just as with automobiles, people in our survey were asked what is important to them when they go out to eat, and the question of most interest to us was whether "healthier food options" is important to their selection. This question allows us to explore what type of person focuses on healthy food options, keeping in mind that this is not as simple as it appears. It's easy to imagine that the complexities and contrary nature of the epidemiological research has pushed some people to tune out scientists and health experts and eat whatever they want.

It's a real limitation that we're asking people about what they do rather than observing what's actually on their plates. Despite this, the eating healthy question probably does get at real differences in behavior. While some people head to restaurants with a salad bar when they eat out, others are much happier with a sixteen-ounce prime rib platter.

In this area, the demographics plus microtargeting model had some success. Two demographic factors were especially key in explaining whether healthy options were important in casual dining selection. Women were much more likely to report this as a factor in their restaurant choices. This is consistent with many purchasing patterns involving food: Women are more likely to buy salads, shop organic, and read diet and nutrition books. Those with more education were also more likely to say that healthy options were important to them.

This decision was one of the few we've looked at where party identification mattered. Perhaps this shouldn't have been unexpected. From the beginning, Americans have been militant about food. In Boston, tea was an early casualty of the Revolutionary War. During the second Iraq war, the ubiquitous french fry was caught up in the hostilities. House Republicans were stirred (but not shaken) in 2003 to change the name in their commissary to "freedom fries" in protest of France's unwillingness to support the U.S. position. More recently, one of the stock tropes of the 2008 presidential election was the difference in diet between red states and blue states. Those residing in the former seemed to live on steak and hash browns; the latter on bean sprouts and lattes. But there is some truth to the clichés: When it comes to eating out, Democrats in our results disproportionately try to eat healthy food.

Even with the importance of these factors, our TRAITS were the dominant determinant of whether a person believed healthy options were very important in choosing a restaurant. The trait that had the most impact was Time. Those who placed a higher value on the future were more likely to say that healthy options mattered. And once again, the higher the score for risky behavior, the less likely people were to say that healthy options were very important. If you're willing to smoke or speed or gamble, you're also more likely to neglect healthy food options and play the health lottery. What, after all, is more important—the memory of a good lunch, or the possibility that you'll need a quadruple bypass in thirty years?

People more concerned with status and the opinions of others as measured by their meToo score are also more likely to say that they consider the healthy options when dining out. It may be that other-regarding people live in a world where you can't be too thin. Even if you aren't thin, it may be worth something to look like you're eating thin. The ability of TRAITS to predict who focuses on healthy food can thus be part of debates about encouraging "socially desirable" behaviors.

As expected, people with high Altruism and Information scores also worried about their health when eating out. Both groups avoid fast food, and both say that they'd reconsider this choice if there were healthier options available.

Last, people who score higher on the Stickiness attribute are less likely to say that healthy options are important in deciding where they eat out. Since these loyal customers are less likely to change brands and experiment with new products, it makes sense that they are less concerned with healthier fare. If you chose your

EATING OUT, EATING HEALTHY

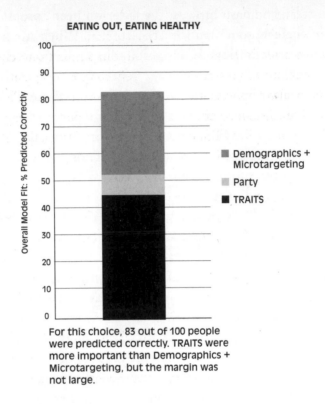

For this choice, 83 out of 100 people
were predicted correctly. TRAITS were
more important than Demographics +
Microtargeting, but the margin was
not large.

favorite restaurant chain ten years ago, healthy eating was less
likely to play a role than it does today.

Like most of the results in this book, we're focused on the
individual. But, it's important to note that choices like where you
eat out aren't made in a vacuum. Customers of different chains
vary widely in their approach to healthy eating in part because of
the choices made by marketers. People who say they visit Burger
King, for example, rarely list healthy options as important to
them and instead focus on the low prices. Some people, however,
began to associate Subway with healthy eating because of the ad
campaign featuring Jared Fogle, a college student who lost over a
hundred pounds in three months by eating a foot-long veggie sub
for lunch and a six-inch turkey club for dinner every day.

After Subway's ads made Jared a cultural icon, sales increased by 18 percent in 2000 and 16 percent in 2001. Our data was collected after 2001, and for those in our sample who chose Subway as the fast-food restaurant they went to most frequently, a majority said healthy options were very important to them. Clearly, the ads had their intended effect, and as we'll see in later chapters it's possible to use TRAITS to conduct very sophisticated ad campaigns.

BUSH APPROVAL RATINGS

If President Bush were a product, what would it mean to be loyal to him? When the *New York Times* wanted to find strong supporters of President George W. Bush in mid-2006, they sent reporter Timothy Egan to Provo, Utah. At the time Bush's job approval rating was 50 percent or higher in only three states, and Utah was one of them. Egan found that in a county where Kerry only got 11 percent of the vote in 2004, people still voiced support for the president even though many disagreed with some of his policies. As a conservative sales manager put it, "I'm against the war in Iraq—and what happened with Hurricane Katrina, well, it was a failure by everybody. . . . I tend to judge a person by their character. President Bush reminds me of President Reagan. He's a man of principle." A student at Brigham Young University offered what Egan called "blanket approval of the president," but when asked which policies she most approved of, said, "I'm not sure of anything he's done, but I like that he's religious—that's really important." The chairman of the Democratic Party in Utah wasn't surprised at all by what Egan found and said that people in the state were "more trusting, more patient with a president."

In our data, we approached Bush's approval ratings by taking two snapshots out of our data set. In essence, we're looking at opinions of Bush at two different points in time and asking the question, who changes? The first snapshot consists of people who told us how much they liked Bush in 2004; the second snapshot comprises people who answered the question in 2005. Given our huge sample, it turns out we have thousands of people in both years. These years bridge a turning point: In 2004, Bush's approval held steady in the low 50s, and he defeated Kerry with 51 percent of the vote. In 2005, however, Hurricane Katrina and a worsening situation in Iraq and Afghanistan pushed Bush's approval ratings down to 40 percent. A lot of Americans outside Provo changed their minds in 2005, so we have a rare opportunity to look at how the different models perform when we know that there's a significant amount of change afoot.

Unlike every other choice we've considered, the factor with the largest impact on how you view the president is party identification, with Republicans much more likely to report that they viewed Bush favorably in both 2004 and 2005. This is an almost criminal bias in our results, insofar as party identification and supporting a Republican president are very, very closely aligned. But it's worth reporting anyway, just to show you that our results make sense and aren't doing damage to reality.

Demographics plus microtargeting also reveal the expected relationships. Blacks tend to dislike Bush, while married people, Fox News viewers, and churchgoers support him. These groups don't change their views much between 2004 and 2005.

Meanwhile, some of our TRAITS had a significant impact on attitudes toward Bush that were consistent from 2004 to 2005. People with high Altruism scores were more likely to view President Bush unfavorably. Conversely, people with high risk acceptance and those with high meToo scores were more likely to say that they had a favorable impression of the president in both years. The relationship with Risk is straightforward; a large part of the Republican platform rests on individualism and an assumption of personal responsibility (e.g., a belief in a more limited federal government and personal investment rather than Social Security). The meToo trait is less obvious, but may indicate that caring about appearances and the opinions of others makes it unlikely that you're going to be an opinion leader and respond quickly to new information. If you chose a network that was biased toward one party or another, you may have a continuing bias against changing your political views due to social framing.

Stickiness, of course, inclined people to stay with the president. To look at this under a more powerful lens, we divided Republicans and Democrats by their Stickiness scores. Republicans who were stickier in the consumer market were more likely to rate Bush favorably. Democrats who tended to stick with the same products were also more likely to rate Bush favorably. Even though they were from the opposition party, these Democrats stuck with the status quo and stood by the president.

Some of our TRAITS, however, capture a dynamic component that other models completely miss. People with high scores on Information *did* budge, and they moved a lot over this time period. In 2004, prior to the election, more information meant more approval of Bush. But starting in 2005, more information meant much, much more dissatisfaction with Bush. Whether it's a president or a soft drink, negative press affects people based on their TRAITS, and the first to react are those with higher Information scores. Note that we aren't saying the president was bad; we're only measuring the effect of negative information (which may or may not be accurate or justified) on a product's appeal.

The second trait that had different effects in 2005 than in 2004 was Time. In 2004, a high Time score had no relationship to Bush's approval numbers. But in 2005, the effect was very strong—higher concern for the future meant lower numbers for Bush.

These same patterns also held when Knowledge Networks asked if the country was headed in the right direction or had gotten off track. Because this question isn't tied to Bush, it's very supportive of our results that explain how people's TRAITS affect their reception of (in this case, bad) news. On a number of different dimensions over the same period, there were increasing problems both domestic and abroad (e.g., in economics, the dot-com bubble bursting and a growing federal budget deficit), but not everyone responded to this information. It took a complex mix of demographics and TRAITS to allow a person to change.

HAPPINESS IS A WARM GUN

Our final results in this chapter look at how happy people are with their material possessions and the quality of their lives. The KN survey asked people how satisfied they were with their cars, houses, neighborhoods, vacations, wardrobes, and overall standard of living. Not everyone is a material girl or boy, and you might quibble that not everyone is defined by their dining room set. But to the degree that a person is *not* motivated by their belongings, we'd expect them to be satisfied with what they have. Put another way, if you find an ascetic meditating alone on a rock in the desert, you wouldn't expect him to start carping about his household furnishings.

The following chart shows the salient factors that determine your material satisfaction, placed on a 100-point scale. On this scale, the entries in white boxes make you happier; the entries in gray boxes make you unhappy. A score that's closer to 100 indicates that the attribute has a large effect on your material happiness, while the effect of those closer to 0 is negligible. You can also compare numbers to see what the relative salience is of the different factors. For example, going to church makes you a little more than two times as happy as owning a gun:

Age	+9 per additional decade over 24 up to 75+
Time score	+29 if future has value
	−29 if not
Income (<$10k = 0 points; up to $50k = +1 points; up to $75k = +2 points; $75k+ = +3 points)	+12 per point of income
Risk score	−20 if acceptant
	+20 if averse
Stickiness score	+35
homeowner	+31
churchgoer	+26
kids	−24
divorced	−21
gun owner	+12
female	−11*
meToo score	+5 if other-regarding
	−5 if not
Party ID = GOP	−8
Altruism score	+4 if other-concerned
	−4 if not
Information score	+2 if info geek
	−2 if not

One way to understand the results in the table is to calculate your own level of happiness. If you've taken the quiz in the appendix, simply go through the table, and for each box add or subtract the number that corresponds to your demographics or TRAITS. The final number is your overall level of happiness, where the bigger the positive value, the more materially happy you are.

In every case, each of the above characteristics makes you happy (or not) across the entire battery of questions. It may

---

* Women are happier with their cars, but less happy with their homes and wardrobes.

surprise you that the Time trait, to take an example, makes you happier not only with your wheels but also with your house, neighborhood, and vacations. The only exception to this is your gender, where we discovered a car-wardrobe divide. This kind of pattern inspires confidence in our results, though not everyone may like that we've confirmed a stereotype.

Finally, our best advice is that if you get a divorce or have kids, go out and buy a house if you don't own one already.

SEEK, AND YOU SHALL FIND

This would be a shorter chapter if we'd found simply that higher incomes and education levels make it more likely that people will get what they want. We find something quite different. After you take into account the many different ways that people vary in terms of age, gender, income, education, and race, there are still readily identifiable patterns in the quality of choices that people make. Once again, your TRAITS define you, and in the examples of this chapter, they tell us how satisfied you are with your choices.

In fact, across the range of choices we've studied here, a profile emerges. People with higher Time, Information, and Altruism scores tend to make better choices, while people with high acceptance of risk are much less happy with their choices. If you are highly sticky, you also tend to make worse choices, but you're pretty happy anyway.

The combination of TRAITS you bring to your daily life can help predict whether you end up healthy, happy, and wise. What actually makes you happy, in terms of how you believe a life should be lived and what the world should be like, is a trickier question that we've only partially answered. In the next chapter, we'll apply our TRAITS to a different question: Who becomes a fan?

4

All-Consuming

We're consuming all the time. When you woke up this morning and had a cup of coffee, you exchanged money for the pleasure and stimulation contained in your mug. While you slept, you were also consuming—the electricity powering your house overnight comes at a price, but you think it's worth it to be able to turn on a light if your baby wakes up at 3 a.m., and to be able to take a hot shower first thing in the morning. Consumption, across the entire range of material possessions from coffee to high-definition plasma televisions, is something we're all familiar with. It's why most of us go to work, and there's a direct relationship between what we're willing to spend on a product or service and the pleasure (or utility) we receive from it.

There's a different kind of consumption, however, that may not be as well understood. We also consume ideas or ideologies, and the relationship between the price we're willing to pay and the pleasure we get from our consumption isn't as straightforward as it is for material goods.

To illustrate what we mean by consuming an idea, let's start with an extreme example where the stakes are very high and your choices might determine whether you live or die. Imagine you're a British officer at the Battle of the Somme during World War I. The battle, which began on July 1, 1916, was fought on a scale difficult for most of us to imagine. As the military historian John Keegan relates, over one and a half million shells were fired at the German trenches in the weeklong buildup to the British offensive. The heaviest artillery pieces—fifteen-inch howitzers—fired shells weighing fourteen hundred pounds each. Almost three-quarters of a million Allied troops participated in the initial attack, each carrying close to sixty-six pounds of equipment and ordered to walk at a steady pace across the no-man's-land between the British and German trenches. Facing them was an array of weapons, but nothing was as deadly as the machine gun:

> A sergeant of the 3rd Tyneside Irish describes how it was: "I could see, away to my left and right, long lines of men. Then I heard the patter, patter of machine-guns in the distance. By the time I'd gone another ten yards there seemed to be only a few men left around me; by the time I had gone twenty yards, I seemed to be on my own. Then I was hit myself."

Put yourself in an officer's boots on the morning of the battle. You know that in some battalions, officers dress like their men (effectively as camouflage), but that in your battalion, silver spurs, riding breeches, and the like are the standard dress. This is in spite of the fact that distinctive uniforms make officers easy targets for the German soldiers who are trained to recognize them and shoot at them first. Even more surprising, however, is that some of your fellow officers are not even carrying a weapon into battle:

> All carried sticks, polished blackthorn with a silver band in the Irish regiments, Malacca canes or ash plants with a curved handle, of the sort sold by seaside tobacconists, in others. Some carried nothing else, not even a revolver, thinking it an officer's role to lead and direct, not to kill.

Since the whole point is to cross no-man's-land and enter the enemy trenches, not having a weapon in close quarters combat is virtually suicidal.

What would you have done? Would you have dressed like your men and carried a weapon, or would you have acted like many of your fellow officers and bought into an ideology where proper officers didn't do these things?

The Battle of the Somme lasted until November 18 and choices like these were made every day. By the end of the battle over four hundred thousand British soldiers were dead or wounded, along with nearly two hundred thousand French soldiers. The German army also suffered terribly, losing roughly half a million soldiers. But of all the groups engaged in this lengthy battle, officers suffered proportionally greater losses than any other. On that first day alone, because of their failure to understand the nature of the conflict combined with an ideology that caused them to advertise themselves as high-value targets, nearly 60 percent of all British officers taking part in the attack died.

The choices made by many of the British officers seem incomprehensible in hindsight, and this is a source of concern for researchers. By and large, social science is founded on the notion that human beings make rational choices. People have preferences, and given the choices and information available to them for any decision, they are assumed to act in their own interests and choose the option that will provide them with the most happiness. In the context of armed conflict, you can be killed if you make the wrong choice, so it is especially surprising to see choices that seem at odds with maximizing your life span. We've seen other choices that potentially have weighty consequences—notably the decision to get a flu shot or not—but none so stark as this.

You might think that the British officers at the Somme did not make the right (or optimal) decisions. Their ideas about military service and class appear antiquated. After all, the modern U.S. Army recruited soldiers using advertisements with the slogan "An Army of One." The muscular heroism of Rambo or the Special Forces soldiers featured in *Black Hawk Down* is much more understandable to us. We might, in fact, go so far as to view the British officers as foolish creatures of a less rational age.

But this would be wrong. The British officers saw marching across a field unarmed, dressed essentially as targets, as perfectly rational. They were living out the belief that, as warriors, they should risk their lives for their ideals and that, as officers, they should leave the killing to the enlisted men. Their distinctive officer's clothing, which they would not alter or hide, identified them as part of an elite and different from those of lower classes whom they commanded. They gained comfort from signaling to other officers on the line that they shared a common identity and had a special calling. Expressing a belief and being part of a social network got them out of the trenches and into no-man's-land, even though they realized the price might be death.

The actions that today seem anachronistic and irrational made sense to the officers, once you factor in how their choices made them feel about themselves and their ideals, forged by their public school and university backgrounds and the British class system. From the perspective of a modern economist, the offi-

cers were not rational, because they did not engage in the opti-
mizing behavior economists assume is ubiquitous. Nor were they
irrational, because their choices were not governed by random,
emotional, or nonsensical impulses. They weren't, in short, making mistakes, they were simply choosing differently.

So if the officers were neither rational nor irrational, how were
they making decisions? And while most of them acted in a way
that put their lives at increased risk, why did some of them decide
to dress like the enlisted men, carry a weapon, and in general pay
more attention to the risks involved in their actions? What happened on the Somme is not so different from what happens in
America every four years, during the presidential election, when
some of us choose to vote and others don't. Though voting and
volunteering seem on the surface easily understandable, they
share much more in common with the seemingly incomprehensible decisions of the British officers than is immediately obvious.
On the surface, one might view both actions as virtuous or as a
duty of citizenship and thus in the domain of the Altruism trait.
The parallels run deeper, though.

Consider how far people are willing to go to participate in
the election. After a bitter recount battle in Florida in 2000, some
voters in the 2004 contest were unwilling to trust voting officials,
according to an October 28, 2004, *New York Times* article:

> Herman Post, who said he divided his time between Connect-
> icut and Boca Raton, said he called the Palm Beach County
> elections office 10 days ago to inquire about [an absentee] bal-
> lot he requested in September, and was told it had been mailed
> on Oct. 12.
>
> When Mr. Post still had not received the ballot [several
> days later], he said, he called back.

"They say they never mailed me one, that there's no record from me having applied for it," he said. "I think there's obviously some phony baloney going on down there."

Mr. Post, 82, said he would drive to Florida to vote, leaving Connecticut at dawn on Sunday.

Clearly, by any measure, Mr. Post was willing to devote an enormous amount of time, money, and energy to make certain his vote would be counted. Many would applaud his actions.

But herein lies the mystery for social scientists. At the risk of sounding cynical, Mr. Post's actions were not "worth" it. Let's imagine he worried about the plight of the poor and this was the issue that motivated him to vote. The time he spent voting could just as easily have been spent working. Instead of spending several days phoning officials, driving to Florida and back, and thinking about his vote, Mr. Post could have cut a check to the charity of his choice in the amount of the wages he would have lost by voting. Given the inefficient government bureaucracy, not to mention the high probability that his candidate would have won or lost regardless of whether he voted in a state with over seven and a half million ballots cast, Mr. Post could have helped the poor a great deal more had he worked and written a check.

Despite widespread indifference to elections, Mr. Post is by no means alone in his extraordinary concern with politics. Moriah-Melin Whoolilurie spent her honeymoon working with Dennis Kucinich's Peace Train in 2004. She was asked by blogger Justin Walker why she supported Kucinich. "'Because he speaks the truth,' she says with a soft, earnest sincerity. 'He speaks to my heart. And his courage has given strength to my voice.'"

Ms. Whoolilurie's words give us an important clue to her motivations. Her choice to spend her honeymoon working on a campaign was not based on any expectation of future rewards. After all, Kucinich had no chance of winning the Democratic primary, much less the White House. There would be no cozy ambassadorship in the Caribbean for Ms. Whoolilurie, nor a tax break for her business. It was about quite different factors involving altruism, self-expression, and becoming part of a group of like-minded people—in all respects, the same motivations that explain the actions of the British officers. But why, when almost half of all eligible Americans do not vote (even when it is convenient) and even fewer volunteer, do some voters go to such extremes and make these types of decisions?

What these two groups—British officers during World War I and extraordinarily motivated voters from 2004—have in common is that they were not engaged in the sort of strict cost-benefit analysis that describes most of our consumption. As an individual officer at the Battle of the Somme, your movement into no-man's-land will not turn the tide. As an individual voter, you're not going to determine who wins an election. Going unprepared into battle or getting to the polls each appears to be a losing proposition. But the officers did march, and voters do assemble, because of additional aspects of these decisions—the way they let you express a value, be part of a team, and affirm an identity. Yet in both cases, not everyone made the same choice. Some officers carried weapons and blended in with their troops. Some Americans never vote and consider it a waste of time.

There is clearly a difference between consuming ideas and consuming material goods and services, and so far we've ignored this distinction. In previous chapters, we've applied our TRAITS to things you can hold in your hand, like flu shots, investment portfolios, or a glass of wine. Yet there is a whole world of decisions that are less tangible but still very important to people.

Our main goal in this chapter and the next is to see if our TRAITS help explain decisions that involve the consumption of ideas. What types of people are most likely to derive positive utility simply from believing in an idea or becoming a member of a team, and how are the rules different when one is supporting the environment rather than buying a movie ticket?

Marching into battle or into a voting booth look like very different decisions until you see that both involve choices that express ideas and identities. Deciding whether to become engaged in politics, live a green lifestyle, or send your kids to public school all have ideological components. We show that these decisions are actually strongly related and, once you know a person's TRAITS, predictable.

CONSUMING THE ENVIRONMENT: IT'S NOT EASY BEING GREEN

You turn off the water while you brush your teeth, you've taken a Prius for a test-drive, and you've installed compact fluorescent light bulbs in your house. But—you still take a twenty-minute shower, refuse to give up those pretty Fiji water bottles, and just can't seem to put your newspapers in that recycling bin.

These are the words that greet you at TrueGreenConfessions .com, a place where people can anonymously post their feelings about how hard it is to live green. The site offers snippets of the modern sins that can lead you astray on the eco-friendly path. There's hypocrisy: "I buy recycled toilet paper and put it in my main bathroom (the one the guest would use). For my own bathroom, I buy the non-recycled cushy stuff." Pride: "I spent $260.00 on stainless steel, eco-friendly, reusable water bottles for my whole family. . . . I think it was more about 'looking green' than 'living green,' because if I really cared, I should have just recycled some milk jugs." Sloth: "I only recycle when the bin is closer to me than the garbage." And hedonism: "Is it okay to recycle my plastic bags but secretly still love to ride my Jet Ski on the river? There are so few pleasures in life."

Why are these greens racked with guilt? If you don't recycle a bottle, the world stays essentially the same. Throwing one additional bottle in the trash won't mean we need to open a new landfill. Reusing a bag doesn't mean we can close an electricity plant. Biking up the hill to work won't halt global warming. Yet in the same way that some people feel a duty to vote, some will heed the call to live green. It could be because they enjoy expressing their beliefs to others. They may derive satisfaction from living out their identity as environmentalists or feel an obligation to future generations and people in other countries. By recycling they end up consuming something extra—a vision of themselves as doing the right thing and helping the planet.

The amount of utility people derive from consuming ideas can be considerable, and if they fail to conform to these ideas, they can also feel pain. Take the Prius, as an extremely visible example. Before the market for new cars crashed in late 2008, the Prius was selling for an average price of almost $27,000, which was above the manufacturer's suggested retail price. Even more shocking, a used Prius with low mileage would cost more than that, due to the shortage in supply of the new cars.

Given the expense of the car, Prius drivers have a lot invested in living the green life, and they expect that their car will get excellent gas mileage. Indeed, *Consumer Reports* found that the Prius has good gas mileage: Depending on the type of driving, the Prius got 35 to 44 miles per gallon. Much to the consternation of Prius owners, however, these numbers were not as magical as Toyota had promised, and the news was full of stories about hybrids' not living up to their gas mileage claims.

The Prius is interesting because even though it is a material good, there is also a substantial ideological component involved in the decision to buy one. The reason news stories about exaggerated mileage claims upset owners was not because of the absolute numbers (which were still quite good), but because we want our ideals unsullied by negative coverage.

All of this, though, is beside the point if you adopt a purely rational attitude and want to save the environment (and as much of your bank account as possible). Instead of a Prius, you could buy a much less exotic car that uses an efficient gasoline engine. The Scion xD and smart fortwo coupe are two vehicles that get mileage in the mid-30s, and either car will only set you back about $15,000. The Prius uses less gas than these cars, but not by a lot—at current prices, the difference is about $300 worth of gas per year.

Putting two and two together, if you opt for the Prius you'll spend an extra $12,000 to save $300 annually. Even if you aren't an investment banker by training, that's not a very good return on your money. If you love the environment, and you aren't consuming the idea of owning a Prius, it's a much better plan to buy one of the small, gasoline-based cars and spend the extra money elsewhere. For this amount of cash, you could buy 120 acres of Amazon rain forest, preserving it *forever*. Or you could be even more direct and just buy carbon credits with the money—about 750 tons' worth. That amount of carbon is huge. It's like waving a magic wand and turning seventy-five Hummer H3s into Prius cars for an entire year.

The problem, of course, is that owning a slice of the rain forest or tons of carbon credits are not visible signals that you love the environment. And you're not reminded every day of your devotion in the same way as seeing a Prius in your driveway. The key to understanding the decision to buy a Prius is understanding who is likely to consume ideas. In this case, consuming the idea costs in the neighborhood of $10,000, but most Prius drivers would say it's worth it.

All sorts of environmental decisions, from buying a Prius to reusing plastic bags to recycling, can be costly. If you add up these actions across billions of decisions made by millions of Americans, the environment can be protected—just not for free. For many of these eco-friendly actions, you bear the cost and society gets the benefit. The return to you comes primarily in how this makes you feel about your actions. If you're an environmental fan, the warm glow from expressing yourself and doing the right thing motivates you to carry the recycling bin to the curb. So what makes some people and not others fans of the environment?

To study environmental consumption, we look at "living green" in two different ways. In the first section, we use a scale that captures the degree a person says she recycles different categories of materials: newspapers, cans, glass, and plastics. In the Knowledge Networks surveys, about half of the respondents report participating in these actions. In the next section, we'll look at the truly devoted consumers of the green life: people who give their money and time to the environment.

RECYCLING

At this point it's safe to say that everyone has heard about recycling. There have been a number of public information campaigns designed to increase participation in recycling programs, and if you aren't recycling, it's because you simply aren't a fan of the environment, are lazy, or don't believe that recycling helps. Fans, on the other hand, are happy to participate and will walk that extra distance to safely dispose of their soda can. It's important to note, however, that it's easier in some places to be this kind of fan because recycling is commonplace and the opportunity costs are so low. In many situations, the only thing that's required is to throw your trash into a different-color bin.

To explain who becomes a fan of recycling, let's start with a model that consists of demographics plus microtargeting. Part of the story of who recycles lies in demographics, but it's not very much of the story. African Americans, gun owners, and churchgoers tend not to recycle, while people who live in urban areas do (most likely because the opportunity costs are lower—recycling bins are more common, recycling trucks arrive at the home more often, etc.). These effects, however, are all relatively slight.

Even after you take demographics into account, the TRAITS play a very large role in explaining who recycles. The benefits of recycling are often far in the future and spread across many people. Individually, no one receives a large payoff for recycling, so you have to care about other people to make it worthwhile. Each of these dimensions affects how people react to the decision to recycle. Accordingly, the Time trait matters a great deal, with the expected result that the more people value the future, the more they recycle. The other large effect is Altruism; the more likely you are to engage in charity work and feel a sense of obligation to others, the more you will recycle.

The meToo trait, interestingly, has a dual role in explaining recycling. One part of being other-regarding is that you care what others think of you, and this means having a nice house, a nice car, dressing well, and the like. None of this predisposes a person to take a lot of pleasure in recycling. The other part of the méToo trait is spending time with other people, and this does predispose a person to recycle. Polls consistently demonstrate, for example, that well over half of Americans support recycling, and this support is even stronger in urban areas. Ultimately, the effect of the méToo trait probably depends on who you know, and whether they're recycling too.

The results of our horse race are displayed in the following graph. As is evident, TRAITS do very well once again, with demographics in second place. One striking outcome is that party identification does *not* matter. Recycling, despite stereotypes, is not the exclusive domain of liberals.

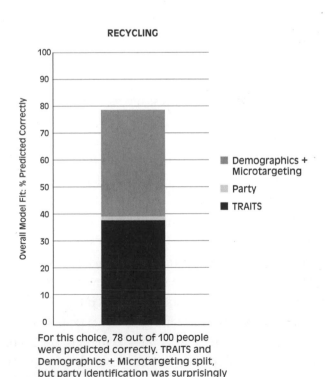

For this choice, 78 out of 100 people were predicted correctly. TRAITS and Demographics + Microtargeting split, but party identification was surprisingly ineffective.

THE GREEN LIFE

Recycling is just part of living green, and frankly it's the easy part. Hardcore greens buy recycled products, reduce energy use, drive cars that generate less pollution, and volunteer their time and money to green causes. There's even a cable channel for people who strongly identify with living a green lifestyle. Planet Green was introduced by Discovery Communications in the summer of 2008 and features shows on everything from how to have an eco-friendly picnic to how to do home improvements that will save the earth and reduce your electricity bill. The idea of the channel is to provide "eco-tainment"; advertisers hope that this focus will help them sell green products. As one media analyst put it, "Green is a category companies want to be in. . . . Whether you're an automaker or a bank or a petroleum company, somewhere in your marketing plan is something referring to the environment."

All of these actions are costly, so the question is: Who devotes the time and resources necessary to be a part of this more dedicated group of fans? To develop a measure of green fandom we combined information on environmental actions that are less frequently observed: volunteering with an environmental group (reported by 3 percent in the Knowledge Networks surveys), giving money to an environmental group (9 percent), buying recycled goods (18 percent), and reducing energy use within the last twelve months (45 percent).

When we look at demographics plus microtargeting, the story is substantially different than it was for recycling. There's no longer any effect for living in a city, owning a gun, or your race. Churchgoers are even less inclined to participate in these activities than they were for recycling, but the main factor is your education level. As education goes up, so too does the chance that you'll live green. Your political party also has a substantial effect here—we find Democrats more willing to become fans of the environment.

Surely these factors matter, but once again not as much as TRAITS. Like recycling, these actions involve paying a price today (for example, a donation or a volunteer hour) for a social benefit down the road. The difference is that time, money, and driving a Prius are more costly than dropping a can into a recycling bin. Accordingly, we find that people who place a high value on the future and score high on Altruism tend to become fans of the environment.

Unlike recycling, we also find that a high Information score helps predict living green as well. Living green involves changing your previous consumer choices, and thus there is a greater informational burden. Nearly everyone knows about recycling, whether they participate in it or not. Joining or contributing to an environmental group and taking the trouble to make "greener" purchasing decisions takes real cognitive effort.

Apple Inc. is savvy to this idea and has started an ad campaign proclaiming that its laptops are the "greenest." Instead of talking about the benefits of the company's hardware or software, the ads instruct consumers about the materials used to make the laptop, the efficiency of the batteries that power it, and even the packaging it comes in. For most computer geeks, these haven't been salient concerns in the past, and it's not a surprise that sticky people tend not to become fans of the environment in great numbers. It requires considerable flexibility to buy a new laptop based on the package it comes in rather than on how powerful it is.

Finally, the meToo trait matters, but again has a dual role. As we saw with recycling, there's a difference between caring about the appearance you make and caring about your friends and family. Because there is a political component, we tried something new with the meToo trait. Leveraging research showing that people identifying with a major party tend to associate with others in their party, we looked at the combination of meToo and your party identification. The idea is that if you are a Republican, you probably have social networks that include lots of Republicans; we saw the same effect at work in the last chapter when we looked at whether or not people still approved of Bush and the direction the country was going in. This is still something of a leap—we don't have a direct measure of who is in your social network—but the effect is strong. If you are other-regarding and political, you even more strongly support the green lifestyle (if you're a Democrat) or not (if you're a Republican).

FANS ARE EVERYWHERE

Even though we looked at two different types of fandom—the fan who recycles because the costs are low and recycling is ubiquitous, and the ardent fan who has made the environmental movement a significant part of her life at much greater expense—we have a hypothesis about the key elements of people who consume ideology. First, to make being a fan worthwhile, your TRAITS should indicate that you gain utility from actions that only have effects in the future (Time), and from helping other people (Altruism). Second, costs matter. True believers in the green movement have an informational burden that recyclers don't—and their Information trait along with their level of education is proof of this. Finally, having a high meToo trait doesn't necessarily make you a fan—it depends on who else is in your social network and what they believe.

In the next chapter, we'll see if these lessons hold for a very different kind of fan: the political junkie. We'll also dig deeper into the relationship between becoming a fan and the price you pay to consume ideas.

5

Consuming Politics

On Christmas Eve in 2007, the Mall of New Hampshire in Manchester is jammed with last-minute shoppers. Outside the main entrance to the mall, thirty-year-old Clint Van Wuffen is standing in the snow with a blue McCain sign shouting, "McCain! Whoo!" as cars drive by. He takes it as a good omen when three successive cars honk their support. Van Wuffen took a month off from work in Arizona to campaign for John McCain and describes his New Hampshire primary work as "a once-in-a-lifetime opportunity. This is a candidate I feel very strongly about." After a shift of sign waving with other volunteers on Christmas Eve, he's headed back to his room in a McCain supporter's home to grab some sleep.

Even uncommitted voters are working hard in the New Hampshire primary. David Schur, a sixty-one-year-old corporate credit manager, is an independent. He's read Barack Obama's books, *Dreams from My Father* and *The Audacity of Hope*. In fact, he's read the books written by all of the other 2008 presidential candidates too. In one weekend, David and his wife, Lynn, hit six campaign rallies. All of the books and all of the rallies have so far added up to the same verdict for both Schurs: still undecided.

For many third-party voters, there isn't the same excitement as in recent elections. Nader hasn't yet committed to run, and even though Bloomberg has hinted at it, he hasn't announced a candidacy either. Third-party supporters find it especially hard to fathom how anyone could feel a strong attraction to the major-party candidates. Back in 2000, when Ralph Nader was running on the Green Party ticket, Michael Moore told a cheering crowd in Madison Square Garden, "[With] the lesser of two evils, you still end up with evil. You don't make a decision because of fear. You make it on your hopes, your dreams, your aspirations. . . . Follow your conscience." This Christmas, Nader doesn't support anyone in particular, but told Politico.com that he respects Ron Paul (a former Libertarian candidate for president). In his mind, 2008 is another "Tweedledum-Tweedledee election that offers little real choice to voters." Some third-party voters obviously agree with Nader. Despite running as a Republican— a designation the other Republicans don't agree with—Paul is raising millions.

These voters present familiar political types. The committed activist who canvasses, calls, waves signs, and contributes. The independent voter who reads issue positions, visits campaign Web sites, and goes to multiple rallies to shop for a candidate. The third-party voter who insists there is no difference between Bush and Gore and happily pulls for the Greens, Libertarians, or Nader.

We have, though, left out the most numerous type of all: the nonvoter. Nonvoters are spending this holiday season shopping for presents, taking vacations with their families, snowboarding with friends, or even volunteering at the local homeless shelter. In chapter 4, we argued that given the costs of voting, the time needed to become informed about politics, and the minuscule chance your sign waving or vote will affect the eventual outcome of the election, political behavior does not make a lot of sense to social scientists (or to many nonvoters).

But yard signs do pop up, volunteers knock on doors, and candidate bumper stickers appear on the back of Ford F-150s and Subaru STIs. That's because many people consume politics, just as others consume a green ideology. It makes them happy because they are expressing opinions and rooting for a team. If they're a fan of either a Republican or a Democrat, part of their life revolves around elections. They form social networks with other, like-minded fans, and the culmination of their efforts is the election night party. Surrounded by the faithful, they watch the results roll in; some are even moved to cheer and pray for their candidate in much the same way die-hard football fans watch a big game. It's also about staying true to an identity. If they believe it is a person's duty to be an active citizen, then learning about candidates before voting is something that affirms their role as an engaged citizen.

Looking at political participation as a form of idea consumption clarifies many things. If you believe voting to be driven by material needs, you'd expect voters to make decisions based on the relative impact of different policies on their lives, or upon reasoned assessments of the leadership of different candidates. But if choosing a candidate is more like expressing a viewpoint, rooting for a team, or fulfilling an identity, many puzzling outcomes in politics become easier to comprehend.

People will often support policies that go against their material interests, or are based on faulty reasoning, or have little basis in fact. This is the question Thomas Frank raises in his book *What's the Matter with Kansas?* From our vantage point, there's nothing surprising about fans rooting for a team that looks very different from themselves. Ultimately, this is what politics (and professional sports and . . .) is all about: becoming a fan and consuming an ideology.

Now that we have a handle on people who consume environmentalism, it's time to take on politics and see if the TRAITS explain who becomes a fan. Potentially, there are three factors that make it more difficult to predict who will consume politics. First, political decisions are relatively rare. Elections do not occur every day, and for many people the presidential races are the only ones that generate real excitement. In contrast, recycling or driving a Prius are choices that fans of the environment make every day, which help them affirm their identity as fans. Second, much of politics remains out of view; it's what you do in the privacy of the voting booth and think about as you react to candidates and policies. In many circles, it's not even considered polite conversation to discuss your candidate. Finally, there's no clear link between your favorite candidate and outcomes in the real world. Even the president, who is probably the most powerful single individual in the world, is difficult to blame for many of our problems—the world is a complicated place, and it's not easy to evaluate whether you voted for the right person or not. In a way, the complexity of determining whether a policy like free trade (for example, NAFTA) really helps the world or not liberates us to root for whatever team we want without much anguish that we might be wrong.

At the end of the chapter, we dig deeper into the tricky issue of costs. Sometimes, consuming an idea costs only your time. But there can be other costs, and the degree to which you "live out" your beliefs will actually depend on the price tag. Talk is cheap. It is relatively cost free to say that firms should be socially responsible or that diversity should be valued, so we'll look to see if people stay true to these ideas when choosing, let's say, how to invest their money, or which neighborhood to live in. Our results will be based on the decisions of a group of people who should be heavy consumers of ideology: professional politicians who live and work in the Washington, D.C., area.

POLITICS AS SPORT

COLBERT: *What appeals to you about the Republican Party?*

CAREY: *I just think Republicans are very, very wealthy people. And, um, if I want to be wealthy and powerful I should hang out with them. If you play with cripples you start to limp. So I don't want to play with cripples anymore. I want to be up with the NBA players, y'know, which is Republicans.*

COLBERT: *Okay. In your analogy Democrats are handicapped and Republicans are tall athletic black men.*

CAREY: *Exactly. That's exactly what it is.*

—Former California gubernatorial candidate and
adult film star Mary Carey, on *The Colbert Report*

Campaign consultants realize that political affiliations are now like brands. As Matthew Dowd, the chief strategist for the 2004 Bush campaign, put it, "Issues don't matter in presidential campaigns, it's your 'brand' values that matter. Voters see their issue through that brand and how they judge that issue is seen through the brand." Defining what the brand means is important because it affects how voters will interpret a label.

When it comes to consuming political ideology, the first

sign you're a fan is that you've chosen a team to root for. In our data, 30 percent of people say they are Republicans, 30 percent Democrats, 20 percent independents, 18 percent have no preference, and fewer than 2 percent support a third party. So far, we've shown that it's difficult to understand fans by looking at only the material benefits of consumption. But this raises a question: Why would anyone who wants to consume politics *not* join a major team? If most of the benefit is found in sharing a worldview, hanging out with like-minded people, and developing an attachment over time, the decision to be an independent seems curious.

We're also interested in the minority that expresses "no preference." Perhaps they buy the economic logic that dictates that political consumption makes no sense. Or perhaps they're disaffected. We'd like to know.

With these two questions in mind, it should come as no surprise that, of these groups, it's difficult to tell the Democrats and Republicans apart when you look at their scores on our TRAITS. If you support a major party, it means you are stickier than most, enjoy acquiring information, and enjoy a sense of belonging. You're also an altruist: Whichever side you choose, you're convinced that you're doing good.

The demographic profile of people who support a major party is also similar—they have higher incomes, are more likely to be minorities, and are older. Of the microtargeting measures, only gun owners and Fox News viewers disproportionately turn into fans, and you don't need a Ph.D. to guess why. None of these effects are large, however, and most of the work in explaining who becomes a fan of a major party is done by the TRAITS.

When it comes to independents, the story changes considerably. These voters are the Holy Grail of political campaigns. Some independents are willing to gather information, consider something (or somebody) new, decide for themselves, and show up on Election Day. Because their minds aren't made up, this choice involves a lot more work than the choice of a straight party voter, who stolls into a voting booth, flips the party lever, and collects an "I Voted" sticker on the way out the door. Who chooses the potentially more laborious path of a political independent?

Pollsters and political consultants can tell you how models based on demographics plus microtargeting help find independents. They are more likely to be male, older, and more educated than average. African Americans, churchgoers, and those with kids at home are less likely to say they're independents. Our results find the same pattern, but overall these determine less than half of what makes someone an independent.

Being an independent depends on more than you could observe from a family picture on a holiday card: TRAITS help us fully understand this phenomenon. If you are highly sticky and worry about perceptions due to your meToo trait, you're extremely unlikely to be an independent. Risk acceptance also matters—if you like risk, it makes sense that you'd be more likely to be an independent. When people evaluate candidates, there's evidence that they consider not only what the candidate says, but also their track record. Someone you've never heard of before may offer you exactly what you're looking for, but you still may vote for a major-party candidate simply because he is a known quantity. If your Information score is high and you concern yourself with the future, you're also more likely to be an independent. Meanwhile, like supporters of major parties, independents have high Altruism scores.

Finally, there are the people who express no preference for one team or another. It's possible that these people are a lot like independents; they just lack the education to know that it sounds better to say you're an independent than that you don't care at all. Or maybe they've taken a lot of economics classes and buy our logic that voting is a waste of time. For example, just over 40 percent of the no-preference people in our sample voted in the 2004 presidential election; of independents, it's close to 80 percent. Neither equals, however, people who root for a major team: 86 percent.

Despite these possible similarities, people who have no preference really aren't fans and are quite distinct from independents, much less major-party supporters. People without preferences are low on Information, have low Time scores that suggest they don't value the future, aren't altruistic, and aren't loyal. In short, they couldn't be more different from the fans of the environment we covered in the last chapter or the Republicans and Democrats in this one.

In contrast, independents are somewhere in the middle. They share similar scores on Altruism and Time with major-party supporters, but their meToo scores indicate they care less about how others view them, aren't very sticky, and are much more risk-acceptant. Put another way, like major-party supporters, they're convinced they're doing the right thing and they care about the future, but they don't get much satisfaction from being part of a team or staying true to a brand.

Our first pass at explaining political fandom is revealing. We can say a lot about who becomes a fan based on the fact that they've chosen a team. But it's worth noting one thing we can't tell you with TRAITS: which party people will ultimately join. One way to think of this is how you'd think of cheering for your favorite sports team. The rosters change, you might move to a new city, *they* might move to a new city, but if (for example) you root for the Steelers, you're going to wave your Terrible Towel no matter what. Modern politics offers some support for this. After all, for voters in the 2008 election, the most recent Democrat in the White House, Bill Clinton, had reformed welfare and was as pro-business as any president in recent memory. And the most recent Republican, George W. Bush, temporarily banned short-selling the stocks of financial firms and began nationalizing the banking industry.

Some experts worry that the brand depends on sticking to a set of policy positions. Antitax activist Grover Norquist, for one, assails Republicans who vote to raise taxes because it dilutes the brand. As he says, "When you have a brand like Coca-Cola, and you find a rat head in the bottle, you create an outcry. Republicans who raise taxes are rat heads in Coke bottles. They endanger the brand." Based on our research, we doubt many people switch teams because of policy changes. Even an occasional rat head or two isn't going to make a fan pick up and root for another team. There's a lot at stake in political consumption, but most of the time it's not a specific policy position that drives a voter to switch allegiances.

WHO'S KNOCKING ON YOUR DOOR?

Neither Bush or Kerry have gotten a flu shot and both said today they won't get one. Ralph Nader also said he wasn't getting a flu shot. Though in his case he doesn't need one because he doesn't come in contact with any large crowds.

—Jay Leno

Being a fan of a political party is commonplace—as we've seen, 60 percent of respondents to the Knowledge Networks survey identified with a major party, which is about the same proportion of people who said they recycle. Die-hard fans, however, do much more than just call themselves Republicans or Democrats—their idea of consuming politics is shared by the Clint Van Wuffens of the world. They wave signs, man the phone banks, and go door-to-door. Dedicated fans donate time and money to their party and have a great deal invested in the candidates they cheer for. Accordingly, less than a quarter of the people in our data engage in this sort of intense political consumption.

When you talk to these consumers, you realize the extent to which their identity rests on politics. Reflecting on the 2008 primary race right after the New Hampshire primary, veteran *Time* magazine campaign correspondent David Von Drehle said:

> This one is special. . . . You have the Clintons, a powerful dysfunctional family—remember they were the ones that spoofed "The Sopranos"—you have this out of nowhere handsome stranger in Obama that is straight out of "Heroes." John McCain, left for dead in a previous episode, roars back to life, and Mitt Romney, who is a dead ringer for John Forsythe. . . .
>
> And then it all ends in this amazing "American Idol" big episode on Super Tuesday. How can you not watch that? My wife had some minor surgery the other day and the nurse asked her if she wanted to just lay there in the recovery room and rest a little bit. And she said, "No thanks, I have to get home and watch 'The Situation Room' [a political analysis program on CNN]."

The early 2008 primaries coincided with the Hollywood writers' strike, when new dramas and scripted programs grew scarce, providing less competition for the political coverage. Even so, many felt the political drama being played out would compete well if the networks were offering new fare. As *New York Times* executive editor Bill Keller put it, "I think the level of interest in the presidential race would be intense even if writers were still churning out episodes of '24' and 'Grey's Anatomy.' . . . It's a defining race for both parties, with a cast of fascinating candidates, some of whom fall into the breakthrough category. There also seems to be a visceral national yearning to turn the page."

On the night of the New Hampshire primary, many political fans showed up to see the analysis on their favorite cable channels. In primetime, CNN garnered nearly 3.3 million viewers, Fox gathered 3.06 million, and MSNBC attracted 1.64 million.

While 8 million viewers showed up to watch election coverage of the New Hampshire primary, that same week an episode of *Grey's Anatomy* (a drama about life in a Seattle hospital) on ABC attracted 17.86 million viewers. And in the weekend after the Iowa caucuses, fewer than half of those in a Pew Research Center survey could name the winners of the Republican caucus (Mike Huckabee) and the Democratic caucus (Barack Obama). As we'd expect, not everyone is willing to engage in this level of fandom.

Being active in politics can take many forms, so we also study these hardcore political consumers by creating a scale that measures their political activity across many different decisions. These included voting, going to a rally, working in a campaign, donating money, contacting officials, and writing a letter to the editor.

Political consultants often treat demographics plus microtargeting as destiny in campaigns, and this approach does help predict serious fans. If you're older and more educated, the odds go up that you'll be attracted to the sport of politics. If you own a gun or watch Fox News, you're also more likely to get involved. Overall, these factors account for a little more than a third of what makes a person a serious political fan.

When we look at our TRAITS, we see that the habits of mind that reveal fans of environmental causes also reveal them here. Altruists are the most heavily engaged in political consumption, followed by people with high scores in Information and Time. Put simply, we have a very easy time using the TRAITS to predict die-hard political fans because the profile of a die-hard fan is exactly the same.

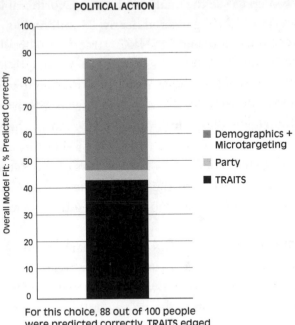

POLITICAL ACTION

For this choice, 88 out of 100 people were predicted correctly. TRAITS edged out Demographics + Microtargeting. Democrats were slightly more likely to become politically engaged.

WILD-EYED BELIEVERS

One thing we couldn't measure for the environmental consumers taking our survey was the strength of their beliefs. Even among those who contribute their time and money to environmental causes, there is certainly a wide range of devotion.

We'd find a lot of these environmentalists in Precinct 31 in Washington, D.C. There are seven Starbucks within a mile, and 81 percent of the latte-loving locals voted for Kerry. It's a place of peace, love, and understanding, unless you drive a Hummer there.

When local resident Gareth Groves brought his 2005 Hummer home he couldn't fit it in his garage (which is not surprising considering he'd paid for extra-large tires and a lift kit that jacked the car even farther off the ground). So he parked it on the street, excited that the car would be part of the "image-based" marketing company he hoped to start. Five days later two masked men broke the windows, slashed each tire, and carved the words "FOR THE ENVIRON" into the car paint. When a *Washington Post* reporter interviewed the neighbors, some were in shock because of the violence, while others thought driving a Hummer was so outrageous that it practically justified the attack.

Clearly there are fans of the environment, and then there are *fans*. You can see this in professional sports as well—Steelers fans wave Terrible Towels. Philly fans throw batteries.

Fortunately, when it comes to politics, we capture policy positions for every person in our survey. We can measure exactly how far out they are on the issues, and determine what factors will predict how extreme political fans are in their beliefs. Part of the answer, of course, lies in demographics. John Zaller, a political psychologist at UCLA, found that the more educated you are, the more ideological you are. He also found that people with a higher level of education more actively filter out evidence that would contradict their existing opinions. If you teach in a college classroom, you can see this in action. More learning doesn't produce moderation—it tends to arm people with the tools they need to preserve their existing opinions.

To look at this question from the perspective of TRAITS, we created two scales: one for moral issues like abortion and gay marriage, and another for economic issues like trade, affirmative action, and taxation. Our question was the same as Zaller's: What causes fans to take extreme rather than more moderate positions on these scales? The way we measured extremism was to look at answers on both of these scales and calculate how far from the center (where the moderate positions are) each person in the Knowledge Networks data was.

For demographics plus microtargeting, we replicated Zaller's work. Education was the second biggest factor overall in making people more extreme. Women and older respondents tended to be less extreme, as did people who were married or had been divorced. Fox News, of course, made people more extreme in our models, though this is quite possibly due to the self-selection inherent in becoming a viewer rather than any radicalizing effect of the network.

As with the rest of our results on consuming ideas, these factors explain a bit less than half of the picture. Meanwhile, three TRAITS matter a great deal in explaining extremism: People with high Information and Altruism scores were much more likely to hold extreme opinions. The single biggest factor overall was the meToo attribute. If you care about how others perceive you, you're much more likely to remain moderate in your beliefs. This suggests that your level of fandom is a race between how much of an information geek and altruist you are on the one hand, and how much you care that other people are starting to avoid you as a nut on the other hand.

EVEN IDEAS HAVE PRICES: DO AS I VOTE, NOT AS I DO, PART 1

We started our investigation of consuming ideas with the example of British officers during World War I. For them, the cost was staggering, but in the modern United States there are few examples where the price of holding an ideology might be your life. It's not the case, though, that the price doesn't matter at all when it comes to consuming ideas. Sometimes, people weigh these prices the same way they do prices in dollars and cents. The question is, what do these costs look like, and when will people give up on an idea because the price is too high?

We've seen one example of this with both the environment and politics. When you get away from simpler activities like recycling or declaring you're a Democrat or a Republican, and move on to more complex activities that involve donating time and money or going off the beaten path and becoming an independent, we're demonstrating the effect of information costs. These more complex activities demand more of a person in terms of both cognition and time, and that's not free. Instead of thinking about whom to write a check to or redeciding in every election which party you're going to support, you could be watching *The Wire*. Usually, more educated people who have high Information scores become fans when the learning burden is high.

Here we explore the price people are willing to pay in their own lives for pursuing an ideology. We're not going to look at just anyone, though. We're going to concentrate on professional politicians who work on Capitol Hill. We can safely assume that if you are a card-carrying member of a major party and your livelihood depends on this affiliation, you most likely have a set of TRAITS indicating that you consume ideas. While we can't measure the TRAITS of legislators and their aides directly, we believe as a group they are likely to be altruists who value information and the future. We can also use their party affiliation to fill in the blanks (since we don't have actual survey responses from these people). As we've seen, people in both parties believe they are altruists, but altruism means something very different for Republicans than for Democrats.

Our first question about legislative staffers is simple: Do they live in neighborhoods that reflect the ideologies they promote? Everyone we're looking at lives in or near Washington, D.C., which makes studying them much easier because they all face a similar decision. "You don't move to DC because it's awesome, you move because it's where your work is." With that blog post, *American Prospect* staff writer Ezra Klein set off an Internet debate about the relative merits of life in D.C. versus cities such as Seattle and Portland. Describing what he himself likes about the nation's capital, Klein said, "Defense wonks and political journalists and Hill staffers and health policy types. It's a city filled with folks I want to talk to. But it's not a city that puts much special effort into being really livable, or pleasant, for such said folks."

Each election cycle there's a new set of staffers coming to work on Capitol Hill who face the same decision as Ezra Klein: to live in the District of Columbia or in Virginia or Maryland. By day, these staffers will eventually work on legislation affecting poverty, crime, pollution, education, and transportation. At the end of the (often long) day, they vote with their feet by going home to the neighborhoods and school districts they've chosen to live in.

You might expect those whose day jobs involve consuming politics to pursue the ideas they advocate in other aspects of their lives. Yet when there's a personal cost to pursuing a political idea, it's not obvious they'll stay true to their ideology. Democratic staffers, for example, place a much stronger value on diversity than Republican legislative aides, so you might expect them to choose more diverse neighborhoods. But if living in a diverse neighborhood is more stressful or costly, as recent work by Robert Putnam suggests, then they might not be willing to pay the price to live in areas with people from many different backgrounds.

Studying a person's housing choice and preference for diversity is tricky. In an era notable for identity theft and political correctness, you're unlikely to get much information by using the *Congressional Directory* to call staffers at work and ask for their home address or their feelings about their neighbors.

So we took advantage of campaign finance disclosure laws to find out where a subset of staffers live, those who contributed to federal political campaigns. The Web site OpenSecrets.org provides data on all contributors who make donations of at least two hundred dollars to federal campaigns. The fact that we're only using people who contributed to campaigns also increases our confidence that we're looking at people who consume ideas and would score high on the Information trait.

Using results from the 2002, 2004, and 2006 elections, we developed a list of contributors who worked for senators, representatives, and congressional committees and sorted them by political party. Though OpenSecrets.org doesn't provide home addresses, the Web site of the Federal Election Commission has the original forms, which do contain addresses. We were able to match contributor names with addresses for 162 staffers. We then used the latitude and longitude of each address to link a person's home with data on the surrounding neighborhood from the 2000 census.

We found that there is a lot of variance in where these Hill staffers choose to live. At the census block group level, a neighborhood size averaging about seventeen hundred people in our sample, the range of housing choices is even more apparent. In the neighborhoods that staffers live in, the percentage of white residents ranges from 14 percent to 100 percent, and the percentage of black residents ranges from 0 percent to 84 percent. One block group had 11 percent college graduates, while another registered 94 percent. The median household income was $77,200 across the block groups, with the highest area having a median household income of $163,000. The block group with the lowest income figure had a median family income of just $28,000. The average year houses in a neighborhood were built ranged from 1939 to 1999.

Despite this variance, staffers who work for Democratic legislators who vote frequently for more diversity are not more likely to live in diverse neighborhoods. Whether you measure neighborhood diversity by race, income, or education, staffers who work to implement very different political worldviews appear to choose very similar neighborhoods. Congressional staffers as a group also choose to live in neighborhoods that have higher income and education and lower percentages of minority residents than the D.C. metro area averages. The party you work for doesn't seem to affect the house you live in.

Democratic staffers live in areas where on average 77 percent of the residents are white versus 79 percent for Republican aides. The average percentage of African American residents is 12 percent where Democratic staffers live, 10 percent for Republicans. The percentage of college-educated residents, per capita income, and average age of house are also nearly identical in the places that Democratic and Republican staffers choose to live. To further test this result, we categorized staffers by the NAACP ratings of the legislators they work for, using these ratings to distinguish between staffers rather than the more blunt instrument of party. Once again, though, our results find that staffers who work for members of Congress with very different NAACP scores go home to neighborhoods that are nearly identical.

Why doesn't political consumption spill over into the "private" lives of these staffers more? Simply put, it's the cost. Whether we like it or not, we often choose neighborhoods that are filled with people we're comfortable with. Congressional staffers tend to have good educations and relatively high incomes; they choose neighborhoods where the residents share these characteristics. And whatever party they belong to, they probably have very similar goals for their children. Thus the choice of where to live is also a choice for many parents of where to send their children to school.

EVEN IDEAS HAVE PRICES: DO AS I VOTE, NOT AS I DO, PART 2

The second decision we examine is how senators and representatives choose to invest their money. Republicans and Democrats take very different stances on issues such as corporate social responsibility and diversity. Do their personal portfolios reflect the difference in ideologies they are appearing to consume in Congress?

Imagine you woke up one morning to discover that you had between $100,001 and $250,000 in stock in the pharmaceutical companies Amgen, Genentech, Novartis, Pfizer, and Wyeth; the defense contractor Raytheon; and retailing giant Wal-Mart. After your morning coffee, you notice that you also have six figures' worth of stock in the oil companies Exxon Mobil, BP Amoco, and Chevron. For most of us, a morning like this would be a dream come true.

For presidential candidate Hillary Clinton, it was a nightmare. In 2001, Hillary and her husband, former president Bill Clinton, had set up a Senate blind trust to hold their stocks and make investments on their behalf. Some legislators choose this route, which keeps them unaware of their holdings, to avoid conflicts of interest. In spring 2007, the Office of Government Ethics told Hillary Clinton that as a presidential candidate she would need to dissolve the trust and make public all her holdings. This trust was valued at between $5 million and $25 million; when it was opened up, the Clintons found out they were stockholders in industries they often criticized. They quickly decided to sell their stocks and place these funds into savings vehicles with lower returns for the duration of the campaign. The price they paid for their ideals was direct.

Most members of Congress don't have blind trusts. They enjoy the same freedom you do to invest in stocks, bonds, mutual funds, or more exotic investments. With this freedom comes another potential choice—deciding whether you care about the social impact of the companies you invest in. Even if you choose a blind trust, you're still free to place restrictions on the types of companies in your portfolio. But becoming a socially conscious investor can entail costs. You may need to monitor the behavior of firms in different policy areas, alter your investments based on corporate social responsibility efforts, and pass up potentially high returns earned by firms that have less than stellar reputations for protecting the environment or treating their workers fairly.

Investment firms have created socially conscious mutual funds and investment plans to cater to people who care about the type of company they invest in. The Calvert Group, for example, rates major companies in five different areas of corporate social responsibility: the environment, workplace, business practices, human rights, and community relations. Firms that score high make it into the Calvert Social Index. Survey data indicate that a minority of investors take corporate social responsibility into account in their investments. The question we are interested in is whether people who consume ideology on a daily basis as members of the House or Senate do the same when it comes to their investments.

Once again, we're using the fact that Democrats and Republicans take different positions on many of the issues measured by the Calvert Group. If you listen to the rhetoric of members of Congress debating the environment or human rights, they sound like fans. They're able to describe why they support (or oppose) regulations to curb pollution or policies to restrict trade with countries based on human rights records. But when you look at how members of Congress cast their investor dollar votes, a different pattern emerges. When it comes to investments, legislators act more like they're consuming a product than consuming an idea.

The 2005 financial disclosure forms filed by members of

Congress tell the tale. If you look at the top fifty companies that representatives or senators listed as part of their stock owner-ship, there's a lot of variance in their portfolios. The list of most popular stock investments for legislators includes firms in many of the industries attacked at Democratic campaign rallies, such as Big Oil, Big Pharma, and Big Tobacco. Despite this, we find that there is no real difference in the stock portfolios of Demo-cratic versus Republican members of Congress. If I know the party identification of a member of Congress, I can't predict that they'll be more likely to buy stock in environmentally friendly companies or any other category in the Calvert index.

We also turned this on its head and looked at the political action committees of the top fifty companies in legislator portfo-lios. When we look at what candidates these corporate PACs are supporting, we find that both Democrats and Republicans invested in companies whose PACs give the majority of their donations to Republicans. So while Democratic legislators vote like fans when they consider bills dealing with the environment, labor, and human rights, when it comes to their own investments their actions are identical to the decisions made by Republican legislators.

LOOKING FOR FANS

The bottom line is this: Consuming an ideology might get you out of the relative safety of your side's trenches to launch an assault across no-man's-land, but you'll still think twice when choosing a school district for your kids or picking stocks.

In the next chapter, we look at the early adopter. If you're trying to introduce a brand-new idea or product, this group is crucial because they'll be willing to buy your product before anyone else.

6

Early Adopters

Comedy may be all in the timing, but if you're trying to predict the success of a new product, there's nothing funny about a slow start to sales. In many markets there is a set of people who are the first to try a new product or idea. In this chapter, we'll see how TRAITS can help you spot who's most likely to stick with the tried and true, and who will be more willing to adopt a new way of doing something.

The spread of environmentalism shows how costly adopting new ideas and products can be. It's not easy being green. Actor Ed Begley Jr. was an early environmental activist in Hollywood and an early user of earth-friendly technologies. Living on the cutting edge of green activism and consumerism, he bought his first electric car in 1970 (on the first Earth Day in America). Describing his Taylor-Dunn electric car, he says, "It was essentially a golf cart. It had canvas doors. It had a tiller instead of a steering wheel. I drove it around L.A. and got the reaction I deserved. People thought it was pretty nutty."

In 1990, Begley put 117 60-watt solar panels on his roof, which captured enough energy from the sun to provide most of his house's electricity needs and power his car. Today his electricity bill is only six hundred dollars a year, but things did not start out smoothly with the panels. Begley says that the "problem was the type of energy they generated. My answering machine and stereo buzzed. The clocks ran fast. The VCR time was kerflooey. I needed a better device to convert the electrical current, which I got, and things have worked out flawlessly ever since."

Begley is clearly an environmental fan, willing to pay a personal price to take actions that have long-term benefits spilling over to many other people. As environmentalist Robert Kennedy Jr. puts it, "Ed has a greater sense of social obligation than anybody I know. He's like a West Coast cadet who gets up every morning and says 'reporting for duty.'"

Begley is also an early adopter, the type of person willing to change his mind and seek out new ideas and products. Everett Rogers popularized the term as a label for consumers willing to take an innovative product or approach and use it before the mainstream catches on and the product gains wider circulation. As we'd expect from our TRAITS, Begley is an early adopter both as a citizen and a consumer. He became inspired by the first Earth Day to volunteer in environmental groups. He went on to head the Santa Monica Mountains Conservancy and the Environmental Media Association and win environmental awards from the Coalition for Clean Air and the Natural Resources Defense Council.

Early adopters can also help us spot trends (or dead ends, if one considers the Betamax, HD DVD, and so far the Zune).

Begley's house offers clues to what you'll be doing to protect the environment down the road. He cooks up vegan specialties on a backyard solar oven, where reflectors can drive the heat up to 375 degrees. The yard itself is surrounded by a white picket fence made from recycled milk cartons. If you bring the food into the kitchen you can serve it on a countertop constructed from recycled Coke bottles. By pedaling for fifteen minutes on his stationary bike in the morning, Begley produces enough electricity for the two and half minutes needed to make toast for breakfast. He's found that fifteen additional minutes generates enough electricity to run his computer for the day.

Not everything about a green lifestyle is ideal. About the compact fluorescent lightbulbs Begley installed, his wife, actress Rachelle Carson, said, "It's horrifying. It's awful. Go look in the dining room. If you're going to do a scientific experiment, you should have this light. But if you're having a dinner party, it's not good."

Begley takes short showers and tries to reduce his wife's water use by knocking on the bathroom door and reporting how many gallons she's wasting by staying in the shower. This particular approach may end up harming the environment. According to Carson, "He says, 'How long are you going to be in there?' I say, 'The more you ask me, the longer I'm staying.'" Begley's environmental quest is comical and continuous enough that he has a cable television program called *Living with Ed* that chronicles his green pursuits. In the show's first episode, he gets a stopwatch to time his wife's showers.

If you look at cast pictures from *St. Elsewhere* or *This Is Spinal Tap* or guest shots from *Veronica Mars* or *CSI: Miami*, there would be no way to predict that Ed Begley Jr. is an early adopter. He's definitely an environmentalist outlier in terms of attention. If you buy recycled merchandise, it's unlikely that your trips to the store will end up in a reality program on cable channels like

HGTV or Planet Green. But Begley's being an early adopter in several domains, such as political causes and cars, is not atypical.

As we'll see in this chapter, TRAITS can predict who is an early adopter in many different areas of decision making. People who love information, don't look to the decisions of others for acceptance or status, have a taste for risk, and are not so sticky that they can't change what they are doing are the early adopters. We'll see how these TRAITS explain who was first in line to buy a Wii, search for news online, or vote for Ralph Nader.

ALL FUN AND GAMES, UNTIL
SOMEONE LOSES A BILLION

When you walk down the game aisle at Target, you're likely to see the smiling face of Mario, the mascot of many of Nintendo's most successful video games. Why is Mario smiling? It could be because in the battle of the next generation of game consoles, Nintendo's Wii console is fast outpacing Microsoft's Xbox 360 and Sony's PlayStation 3. Success in the gaming world can mean a product that ships millions of units, generates billions in sales, and becomes a household word, like the Wii. The danger in playing in this fickle market, however, is the large development cost that goes into designing the game console.

In its 2008 annual report, Sony announced that it had lost nearly $3.3 billion on the PlayStation 3. In part this is because the company had to sell the console at $599, below its production cost. The reasoning for this is simple—if the console takes off and becomes wildly popular, driven in part by its affordability, software sales will climb and production costs will drop. Yet following this strategy involves a bet on markets, technology, and potential customers. The company's annual report warned investors that "the large-scale investment required during the development and introductory period of a new gaming platform may not be fully recovered." If the PS3 takes off, software sales and production efficiencies will eventually yield profits. Yet the report warned that this would not happen if the gaming console "fails to achieve such favorable market penetration."

TRAITS cannot help you solve manufacturing puzzles in the game console industry. But we can provide insight into which people are likely to be early adopters in the market for game consoles. To show this, we'll turn to a unique data source we developed for this book—a mash-up of information from Amazon .com and voting records from a state board of elections.

Amazon makes it easy for you to let your friends know what you would like to buy (or receive as a gift) by adding items to a Wish List with your name and city. Some people will post a single book or CD that they're hoping for. Others will take the time to post a detailed list of books, CDs, DVDs, jewelry, clothes, home furnishings, and other items that Amazon sells. Like much of the data on the Internet, this is a list of intentions. We do not know what a person posting an Amazon list actually has in his library of books or DVDs, but we do know what he'd like to add to his collection.

The Amazon data provide a fascinating window into the products people pine for. You can go online right now, give the site a name and state, and see how the desires of Pauls in California differ from the interests of Pauls in Minnesota. Put in the name of a fort or APO, and you can see what soldiers stationed in the United States or abroad are hoping to listen to or read. Experiment with names in your hometown to see what the neighbors are looking to consume. Google means it's never been easier to keep up with the Joneses.

By querying the Amazon site, we captured the set of Wish Lists on Amazon for people who indicated that they lived in

North Carolina. We chose that state in part because it is our home, but also because the North Carolina State Board of Elections offers anyone with twenty-five dollars the opportunity to buy a CD with the voter registration records of state residents. By matching the names and cities of the Wish Lists with voter registration records in the state, we created a data set that links a person's product desires from Amazon with demographic data such as age, race, gender, and party registration. Our analysis focuses on a clearly defined subset—people in North Carolina who have posted Wish Lists and who have registered to vote. You could easily expand this analysis to your state, however, given the availability of voter registration lists in other states (though other states may charge more than ours for the data).

In chapter 7, we'll describe in more detail how this combination of product and political information could be used to model what customers are interested in. For this chapter we've used the data to focus on predicting who is an early adopter in the gaming console market. Since the Amazon Wish Lists record when people added a particular product, we used the data to travel back in time to the introduction of three next-generation consoles: the Xbox 360, PlayStation 3, and Wii. Not everybody asks for the new products immediately. In fact, during the time period we examined, most people were asking for established game consoles such as the PlayStation, PlayStation 2, and Xbox. To isolate the early adopters, we asked the question: If you're in the market for a game console, what factors will predict whether you're asking for the latest model?

From the voter registration data, we know the age, gender, and race of a person dreaming about a console on Amazon. Totting up the items on his Wish List, we're able to say what percentage of a person's requests for gifts are books. We use this to measure his desire for information. We also created a Bling index, defined as the percentage of Wish List items that fell into categories such as jewelry, watches, and home furnishings. A concern with material possessions and appearance plays a strong role in the meToo factor, so we use this Bling count as a proxy for it. We also included as a control variable whether someone is asking for other high-tech products such as HD DVD or Blu-ray players and disks.

Our rough proxies for the TRAITS do help us predict who's a leader and who's a follower in the gaming market. For those who posted a game console on their Wish List, the people who are high on Information were more likely to ask for the next-generation console. Those high on meToo were also more likely to take the leap into a new system. These relationships held true for all of the next-gen consoles: the Xbox 360, Wii, and PlayStation 3. The high-tech interest predictor complemented these findings; those requesting HD DVD or Blu-ray products were more likely to get the latest in gaming consoles.

In the case of early adoption of ideas or actions that are not widely visible, we'll see that early adopters usually score low on the meToo factor. They don't look to the decisions of others for validation or imitation. For a product like a game console that is shared with and viewed by others, however, it appears that those who adopt early are those who do care about having possessions that convey status and achievement. If having the latest tech toy gives you the satisfaction of showing others you're on the cutting edge, then we would expect those who care about perception and possessions (as measured by the meToo factor) to be early adopters.

Note that a person's political party had no influence on whether he wanted the next generation of game consoles. Stories of political microtargeting often stress lifestyle or product differences among Democrats, Republicans, and independents. Yet without an underlying theory of why these differences should arrive, these correlations do not have much to tell you about the relationship between products and politics. Here we would expect that Information and meToo are the driving forces in who wants the latest console, and that political party should have no impact on this decision. Our mash-up of Wish Lists and voter registration shows that this is the case—whether you're a blue stater or red stater does not determine if you want the Wii.

THE ON-RAMP ONLINE

> kevinrose done with meetings for the day! woke up at 5AM this morning, so a bit tired—now for dinner and a glass of vino w/the girly

That's a note that Kevin Rose sent out on Twitter, a social networking service that allows you to send out text-based updates to friends. These "tweets" have a maximum length of 140 characters, which means Twitter serves as a cross between a microblog ("Here's what I'm thinking") and a group e-mail list ("Who wants to grab lunch?"). Kevin Rose was the 657,863rd person to sign up for Twitter, allowing other users to sign up to follow his tweets via the Web, instant messaging, or text messages on cell phones. As the founder of the social bookmarking site Digg, Kevin is a well-known tech entrepreneur who's already landed on the cover of *BusinessWeek*. So when he sent out his update about dinner and wine, it went to more than forty-eight thousand people who'd signed up to follow his messages (which average about five per day).

The uses of Twitter reflect the different types of information people need. Comcast and Dell use the system to respond to customer service problems. Barack Obama tweeted to provide updates on his campaign, such as, "Honored to be endorsed by Al Gore in Michigan tonight. Watch live streaming video at 8:30pm EST at my.barackobama.com," and "Thanking Hillary. Our party & our country are stronger because of the work she has done."

Most users send messages that are more personal than political. Michelle Slatalla signed up hoping Twitter would be a quick way to communicate with her three daughters. Her early messages included "car pool dilemma will French horn and trombone both fit in mini," "what do you want for dinner," and "found a $20 bill does it belong to anyone." She found, however, that if you tweet them, they won't always come. Only the last message generated a response from her daughters, with one calling to suggest that her mom use the service less and get out more.

Since many Twitter users are tech savvy, they use the term "early adopter" frequently in discussing the growth of the service. In a post entitled "Social Media early adopters," San Francisco Internet analyst Jeremiah Owyang wrote:

> I've seen the social media community run from tool to technology quicker than you can say "shiny object." I've seen us run from blogs > Facebook > Twitter > Pownce > Jaiku > Justin.TV > Ustream > Digg > Delicious > Upcoming > Flickr > YouTube > SecondLife > Widgets > Utterz > Zoomr > Friendfeed > Plurk > who knows what's next.

The chart plotting a count of Twitter users versus time began to look like a hockey stick in spring 2008, with the number of people using the system rapidly taking off. On April 9, 2008, tech blogger Robert Scoble declared, "Anyone who joins Twitter after today is not an early adopter. So, not interesting for me to follow."

Twitter does have strong network effects, meaning that the value to you of using the product rises as the number of users increases. If you're trying to decide whether to adopt a new social media technology like Twitter, you need to think about whether others are likely to join the network and the advantages of establishing a user presence early. As Stan Schroeder wrote about Twitter in a post entitled "The Importance of Being an early Adopter":

> Early adopters tend to exert greater and greater influence on the network over time. Which means it's like a little social pyramid scheme: If you're late, you're screwed. There's a good side to this, of course. It means if you catch new social networks early and stick with them, over time you too will become more and more influential. It means that if you're willing to spend some time trying out new stuff, in the end you'll get rewarded.

Yet there is also the chance that the new product picked up by early adopters won't make it into the mainstream. Even as more people began to tweet, a backlash arose and raised questions about whether the product would gain wider acceptance. As an article in the *Wall Street Journal* about social networking services like Twitter put it, "Some users are starting to feel 'too' connected, as they grapple with check-in messages at odd hours, higher cell phone bills, and the need to tell acquaintances to stop announcing what they're having for dinner."

Survey anonymity means that we can't e-mail the people in the Knowledge Networks survey to see who's tweeting now. But we can explore who was an early adopter online in the KN sample by looking at who reported in 2004 and 2005 that they were searching for news on the Internet. Demographics tell part of the tale. People who are younger and more highly educated are more likely to say that they are online and looking for news. Those with more income are also more likely to be early adopters in surfing for news.

As the graph below shows, TRAITS matter about the same as demographic and microtargeting variables in predicting who is an early adopter in online news markets. Understandably, those who score high on Information are much more likely to be in the early crowd to search for news online. Those whose product choices are sticky are less likely to be early adopters here. Given that news is most often about the actions and fates of others, it is not surprising that the higher your Altruism score, the greater the probability you're online searching for news. The general link between Altruism and political activity carries over into a greater search for news by those who are interested in their communities.

Two other TRAITS point in the expected direction, though the statistical associations are not as strong. If you're high on me'Too, looking to the decisions of others, you're not going to be a trailblazer on the Internet. If you like to avoid risk, you're also less likely to show an early willingness to search for news online.

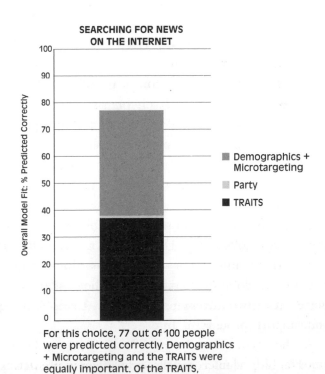

SEARCHING FOR NEWS ON THE INTERNET

Overall Model Fit: % Predicted Correctly

- Demographics + Microtargeting
- Party
- TRAITS

For this choice, 77 out of 100 people were predicted correctly. Demographics + Microtargeting and the TRAITS were equally important. Of the TRAITS, Information mattered the most by far.

Very similar patterns hold in predicting which people in the KN sample said they used the Internet for shopping or went online for financial advice, at times when these actions were less frequent than they are today. Though we often simplify the search for information by describing it as a product of education and income, our results show that even after you control for these demographic factors there is a great deal left to be explained in predicting who goes out of their way to search for information. Our ability to identify who has a high preference for information means that the TRAITS model can predict more accurately who will be an early adopter in online markets for news and for financial information.

LIFE ON THE (POLITICAL) EDGE

On Republican debate platforms in 2008, Texas representative Ron Paul often found himself on the physical and ideological fringes of discussions. Taking lonely political positions was not a new phenomenon for Paul. One analysis of the 3,320 legislators who served in the House of Representatives from 1937 to 2002 determined that Paul was the most conservative Congress member during that period. During one session of Congress (1995–97), he made two-thirds of all the lone "No" votes in the House. Like the die-hard followers of Dennis Kucinich, the Ron Paul faithful viewed their candidate as ahead of his time in staking out clear positions in domestic and foreign policy. As one Ron Paul supporter described the campaign's ability to mobilize contributions and support through the Internet:

> The early adopters are the influential visionaries who recognize the technology for its potential to revolutionize the way

business is done. . . . They are highly motivated and will do what it takes to make their vision become a reality. In the political system, these are the activists. They're forming groups, painting signs, donating money, reaching out, and doing everything they can to spread the message. The visionaries are most definitely going to vote in primaries. They're going to tell their friends. They're going to go to the ends of the earth to make sure their vision is a reality. This is currently where the bulk of Ron Paul's support is coming from.

If TRAITS truly operate across different types of decisions, the same factors that predict who is an early adopter in choosing products and lifestyles should also do well in explaining such political choices. There's no set definition of what an early adopter in politics is, but a willingness to take positions that go against the grain but later may be adopted by the majority could be one. Given the long history of political ideas starting on the fringes of third parties and then migrating toward the major parties, you can look at today's third-party voters as political early adopters.

Third-party followers are a rare and distinctive life-form in American politics. The 2000 presidential election saw candidates from the Green, Reform, Libertarian, Constitution, and Natural Law parties, but together they netted less than 5 percent of the vote. In the Knowledge Networks surveys the relatively small number of voters who said they voted for a third-party candidate in 2000 or 2004 exhibit very different core TRAITS from Democrats, Republicans, and independents. Third-party adherents score much lower on the meToo factor, which captures how much a person looks to the brand choices of others and likes products that make him feel accepted. Just as they're willing to go against the decisions of others in consumer markets, third-party loyalists are willing to make a political choice that stands out. People who are less loyal in product markets are also more likely to try something different in politics, such as voting for a third-party candidate.

Other TRAITS help identify the relatively small fraction of voters who pull for a third party, though their statistical association is weaker. This is for two reasons. First, there aren't that many third-party voters in our sample, and those that are present are members of ideologically distinct parties (for example, Greens and Libertarians). Second, idiosyncratic events affecting the electoral system are likely to impact third parties more than the main parties—for example, Nader's role in the 2000 election probably impacted third-party support in 2004.

Even though our omnibus model fared poorly relative to other choices, a few trends are clear. Those who score higher on Information and have a taste for risk tend toward third-party voting. Meanwhile, demographics do matter in expected ways. Third-party voters have more education, lower income, and are less likely to have children (or guns). Yet, being an early adopter in politics is only partly explained by the demographic and microtargeting variables used by political consultants. Despite the complexities in modeling third-party choice, the best bet if you want to find people willing to vote for third-party candidates is to use the TRAITS model and build on evidence from how they shop, buy, and drive.

DO YOU FEEL LUCKY?

Stories about products that succeed in a market are often told as tales of luck. Yet if you can find out more about the reaction of the likely early adopters of a product, you have a better chance of designing and delivering something that will strike a chord. A perennial question is how to identify and reach those likely to first give the product a chance. In this chapter we've seen that TRAITS improve the odds that you can find the early adopters. Whether we're looking at the adoption of a product, behavior, or idea, our TRAITS predict who tries something new.

People with a greater taste for information are more likely to be early adopters, perhaps because their search for information means they're more likely to learn about new things. People who stick to the tried and true are less likely to try something new. Those with a willingness to take risk are willing to give a new idea or action a chance. For material goods like the Xbox 360, people higher on the meToo factor were more likely to get the new product first. If you care about possessions, appearance, and status, having the latest technology can be important. For things that are less visible, like political ideas or searching online, early adopters are more likely to be those who don't look to others for guidance.

In the next chapter we'll examine how the TRAITS can help you with other decisions that are often seen as the province of luck: poker, advertising, and love.

7

Traits in the Wild

In this chapter, we're going off the beaten path and into the wilds of decision making. Looking at traditional surveys, like the Knowledge Networks data we've been using to demonstrate most of our results, can only tell you so much about people. In this chapter, we're going to use even more immediate information on the way people make choices. With Amazon .com, we'll examine the actual purchasing decisions people make and look for evidence of TRAITS in the type of hardware and software they buy. With Google, we'll see if TRAITS can be used to manipulate the success rates of online advertising. And with a study of Duke undergraduates we conducted, we'll look at how TRAITS can predict betting and learning behavior in poker, and attitudes toward dating and marriage.

The advantages of studying decisions in the wild are twofold. After chapter 2, you might have the idea that we're hard-bitten cynics, and that it takes a lot to convince us that any model of decision making is accurate. You'd be right. To the extent it was possible, we wanted to use our TRAITS model to peer into the real decisions people make in as many different areas of their lives as possible. It's important to step outside the laboratory (even the virtual lab of looking at data) and see if people in the real world are behaving the way your model predicts. For all we know, our results might be limited to the artificial world of the Knowledge Networks data. In this chapter, we step outside that world with new sources of data, and even go so far as to run a miniature advertising campaign of our own to see if we can change human behavior using TRAITS.

The other benefit is that we're studying real choices, rather than attitudes about choice. There's always the risk that people tell you what you want to hear when you ask them about their decisions—they say they vote, or they say they got a flu shot because they believe that's the response the men in the white coats expect. We wanted to sidestep this problem and apply our TRAITS as directly as possible to purchasing, poker playing, and dating.

Along the way, we hope that you can use this collection of results for fun and profit.

TEXAS HOLD-'EM FOR FUN AND PROFIT

Mentally [a job in finance] is less draining than poker. The fundamental reason for this is that you can't lose [your own] money at work. You might make a few terrible trades and

not get paid anything, but it's different than the mental
drain of losing 20% of your net worth in a night. That being
said, trading is by far on the higher end of stressful jobs, but
in my mind it's not as stressful as full-time pro poker.

—Jason Strasser, on the twoplustwo.com forums

Duke University, where we teach, is famous for many things. Our business, law, and medical schools are among the best professional programs in the country. The undergraduate college and many of the graduate programs are also ranked in the top twenty. Even the sports are good: Our men's and women's basketball teams consistently rank nationally. We also have another ranking that isn't as well known: We were home to Jason Strasser, ranked by *Inside Poker* magazine as one of the top three poker dropouts of 2008.

Strasser made a name for himself while he was a biomedical and electrical engineering double major at Duke. While most students spend their undergraduate years going to frat parties and camping outside Cameron Indoor Stadium for admission to basketball games, Strasser played poker. Instead of a summer internship, he went to Vegas and played professionally. It's difficult to know how much money he made because of how often he played online, but his tournament winnings for 2006 and 2007 constituted over a quarter million dollars. He was even written up in the alumni magazine in a story that's typical of the gambling genre. Like the Tibetan monks who practice g Tum-mo and can lower their metabolism, change their body temperature, and perform other mystical feats, Strasser can play four games of Texas hold-'em simultaneously, and isn't distracted even though he's in the middle of a college dormitory. And of course, he can't tell you how much money he's winning. But the story implies it's a lot.

Poker hasn't just swept college campuses, it's also swept America. At any given hour of the day, multiple cable channels are showing professional tournaments, celebrities like Ben Affleck have embraced the game, and there's no shortage of stories about people like Strasser who come out of nowhere to make it big.

Even the geeks are in on the action. A team of artificial intelligence researchers at the University of Alberta have built a poker program named Polaris. Polaris isn't for amateurs—in the most recent man-versus-machine tournament, the program came out on top by beating a team of professional human players. As with everyone else, Polaris's game of choice is Texas hold-'em.

Simply put, if you're interested in human decision-making, you're probably interested in poker. From the beginning, poker was a source of inspiration for a great deal of modern economic theory. John von Neumann, the famous mathematician, member of the Manhattan Project, and inspiration for Stanley Kubrick's Dr. Strangelove character, invented game theory because he wanted to understand poker. With Oskar Morgenstern, he wrote the seminal book *A Theory of Games and Economic Behavior*, which included a model of poker. Generations of mathematicians have studied the game, including John Nash, the schizophrenic genius played by Russell Crowe in the movie *A Beautiful Mind*.

To the extent that you care about bluffing, strategy, and the role of private versus public information, poker is an important game. And if you play poker, you probably want to win. Even if you're only a casual player, you know that there are two facets of the game. The first concerns the odds—with every hand, you can calculate what should happen given the information that's available to you. The second concerns the psychology of the people you're playing against. "Tells," for instance, are tics that give away a player's thoughts. For example, if someone exhibits a lot of bravado, they've most likely got a weak hand and are trying to compensate. Even online, you can look for tells that involve things like the speed of a player's bets. More generally, though, you can try to exploit patterns in decision making that give away information about your opponents.

No data set is complete, so we decided to gather our own. To study poker (and a number of other questions in this chapter), we created a survey that measures TRAITS along with other variables we're interested in. At Duke, we have a captive population of undergrads, and they were the participants in this survey.

We begin with two hypotheses about how TRAITS relate to poker. First, we'd like to know if a higher Information score makes you a better poker player. Of all the attributes measured by TRAITS, we'd expect this one would play a key role in exploiting the mathematical side of the game. Second, we'd like to know if there are attributes that incline you to play in a way that could be exploited by other players. Risk acceptance, for example, probably indicates that you will bet more than the odds would dictate.

As a plausibility test, we first asked the Duke undergrads in our study how frequently they played poker. As expected, we found that men play more often than women, but this effect is dwarfed by the impact of Risk and Altruism. People who like risk play more poker than those who don't, and altruists see poker as the work of the devil. These results aren't surprising, but they do bolster our confidence that we're not inventing something that isn't there.

Our next tests were more subtle. We presented our group of undergrads with actual poker hands and asked them to tell us how they'd play. Ultimately, what you bet says a lot about you, and we can look for patterns in betting behavior that are explained by TRAITS. The following question gives you a taste of what our survey looked like for a very simple game where each player has a single card and the highest card wins:

You have a hundred dollars and are facing one opponent; high card wins.

 VS.

Do you:

1. Fold
2. Bet $0
3. Bet $25
4. Bet $100

This is not a very subtle question, but we saw a huge amount of variance in the answers anyway. You might have determined that an 8 is exactly in the middle of the range of cards, and thus you have a fifty-fifty chance of winning. This isn't anywhere as complicated as a game like Texas hold-'em or Omaha, but it does provide information on whether or not your TRAITS influence your play. To calibrate our results based on experience, we included the frequency that you play poker along with demographics in all of our results.

For this simple problem, playing a lot of poker doesn't change how much you'd bet. It makes sense that if you have a group of reasonably clever people (which we hope our students are), they can use their fingers if need be to figure out that an 8 gives you even odds of winning. What does matter, however, are your TRAITS. Risk acceptance means you bet more, as does a high score on Information and the meToo attribute. We saw these same trends when we looked at poker in chapter 1. Even though we've changed the game and we're looking at a different sample of people, the TRAITS have the same effects.

Our next test involving poker looked at learning behavior. We asked players to evaluate several hands of Texas hold-'em, and gave them a clue about how to evaluate how good their hands were. Hold-'em is reasonably complex, and not everyone can determine the odds of winning. Each player gets two cards down, and then everyone shares five face-up cards. The goal is to make the best five-card poker hand possible. Imagine your down cards are either:

 **or**

It turns out that both hands have about a 16 percent chance of winning, but most people who are new to poker would probably wildly overestimate how good the pair of 10s is compared to the king-10. If you don't play much poker, you may not know that the king-10 is awfully good, since you can create both a possible straight or flush with these cards. We looked at how well people calibrated their bets to the quality of the above hands.

For this more complex problem, demographics and most of the TRAITS didn't predict success. What did, however, was a combination of experience with poker and the Information score. Like other decisions we've studied that involve learning, it takes two things to make a good choice. You have to have some experience with the choice, and you have to have a style of decision making that processes this data. Poker players with low Information scores did very badly at evaluating the above hands—they much preferred the pair of 10s. Only the poker players with high Information scores saw the hands as virtually even.

If you want to win at your local poker table, you may not be able to see tells. Even casual players go to some lengths to avoid giving them away, and if you watched the famous poker scene in *Casino Royale*, you know that some players can even pretend to have a tic when they don't to mislead you. Other players, like Strasser, wear noise-canceling headphones or sunglasses to isolate themselves from the other players.

But you may well be able to guess the TRAITS of your friends and adversaries. If you can, work questions from our appendix into the conversation—"So, have you had any speeding tickets lately?" Or keep an eye out for the guy who shows up on a motorcycle or who can't stop talking about his favorite book. If you can pin down high-information or risk-acceptant types, you can use this knowledge. When they get hands that are good (but not great), you can guess they will bet too much. If dealers call the games so there's a lot of variety in what you're playing, you can also predict who learns from experience, and who is likely to misjudge the quality of their hands when there's a game with wild cards or other complexities.

HOW TO GET AHEAD IN ADVERTISING

We've just seen that you can manipulate your friends at the poker table. Our next question is whether or not you can manipulate your customers and increase the effectiveness of an Internet ad campaign.

Whenever you do a Google search, a set of ads sits to the right of your results. These aren't randomly selected; rather, the advertisements are matched (using an algorithm known only to the brain trust at Google) to your search terms. People bid in an auction for the right to match their ads to your search terms, and every time someone actually clicks on an ad the advertiser pays Google a fee. As a result, some search terms are much more expensive than others. For example, the *New York Times* found that lawyers who are looking for cases are willing to pay dearly for their names to pop up when people with potentially lucrative cases are searching for legal advice. Advertising next to the search results for "asbestos attorney" went for $51.68 in October 2007, and "Oakland personal injury lawyer" brought $58.03. Firms were less willing to spend for searches with lower financial stakes. The term "Christmas recipe" brought only 54 cents, and the (overexposed) Britney Spears brought only 36 cents as a search term.

Our second exploration of TRAITS in the wild uses Google AdWords to test the effect of our model in advertising. It's difficult to determine a person's TRAITS from an anonymous Internet search, so our test is necessarily blunt. But then the Wright brothers' first flight only lasted twelve seconds, so we're hoping you think of this as proof of a concept. We bought searches dealing with movie reviews and lead tests for children (especially in older homes, there's the risk that small children will eat paint or other building materials that contain lead). The group of people who use Google for movie reviews are probably selected at random with respect to their scores on our Risk attribute; the group, however, looking for lead tests is probably more risk-averse than the average Joe. For each of these groups, we provided two different ads. The first is whether or not you want to click to see a biography of Obama; the second asks the question, "Is Obama too risky?"

Our hypothesis is that if people searching for lead tests are risk-averse, then they will be more likely to click on our risky ad frame than the people searching for movie reviews. People looking at the reviews won't disproportionately respond to the framing of Obama as a risky candidate.

We ran our ads for a week and were thus able to look at the searches of thousands of people to test our hypothesis. What we found was that we were mostly right—people looking for lead tests to safeguard their children were much more susceptible to our risky ads than anyone else. There is a word of caution, though. We don't know anything about the people who are searching, and we were only able to test for one trait. We also can't control for the medium of our message (Google on a Web browser), and for all we know there was something in the water during the week we did our test. That said, it's an encouraging first step that indicates you can sell a product more effectively using TRAITS, if you know something about the distribution of TRAITS in your audience.

I'M A MAC. YOU'RE A PC. (AND THIS MEANS I'M WAY COOLER THAN YOU.)

Apple Inc. has always been cool. In the third quarter of Super Bowl XVIII, the commercial that launched a thousand ships was aired, and it had so many layers of coolness it was ice cold. It was directed by Ridley Scott, of *Alien* and *Blade Runner* fame. Tens of millions of people saw it, and then it was never shown again. And there's the enormous good luck that the year was actually 1984, which was serendipitous, since the theme of the ad was that PC users were unwilling participants in an Orwellian nightmare and that the Mac would free them. This was the ad that launched the first ever Macintosh computer.

Today, Apple's war against the PC continues with the "I'm a Mac" ad campaign. A cool, attractive twenty-something is a Mac and a balding, polyester-clad forty-something is a PC. It's not subtle, but by using human actors who pretend to be pieces of hardware, Apple is making the claim that you are what you compute with. In one of the better ads, the PC is bloated almost beyond recognition, and he says it's because of all the useless software built in to a Microsoft system. He waddles around and complains about how he's slowed down. The trim Mac actor sympathizes, sort of.

Microsoft didn't take the latest campaign sitting down, and responded with a brilliant riposte. Their campaign was named "I'm a PC," and the ads start with a dead ringer for the actor Apple used to mock PC users. He says, "I'm a PC," and then a crowd of people follow him: astronauts, lawyers, environmentalists, and bloggers for Obama and McCain. There's even Tony Parker, Eva Longoria, and Deepak Chopra. The message in these ads is that all of these people do real work with PCs and are successful. In a sly way, it points out that the Mac ads are mostly about image, and that image is not as important as accomplishments.

So who buys a Mac or a PC? And are these commercials successful in targeting different types of people? We looked at two sources of data to examine the differences between Mac and PC users. The first is the Amazon data we used in chapter 6; the second is the survey we used to look at the TRAITS of Duke undergraduates. These are very different sources of data, but we found that there are systematic differences between Mac and PC users in both of them.

The Amazon data has limitations, and as we discussed in the previous chapter, we can only look indirectly at two of the TRAITS: meToo and Information. While we can't look at every trait, we can, however, look at tens of thousands of people and their desires for products—in this case, whether they want Mac or PC products on Amazon. It's easy to distinguish products because Apple products are in most cases distinct from PC hardware and software. What we found was that men preferred PCs;

this effect wasn't huge, though. Other demographics plus micro-targeting variables didn't factor into this decision—your race and party identification, for example, don't allow us to guess whether you're a Mac or a PC.

What did allow us to guess your preference was the large effect of the meToo score. In the Amazon data, we measured this trait by looking at how much you spend on home furnishings, jewelry, watches, and other types of bling. If you care about appearances, you probably own a Mac. What didn't matter was your Information score. Information geeks were equally likely to choose a Mac or PC, which suggests the choice isn't about the merits of the hardware.

The survey data using Duke undergrads is much more precise; they took an extended version of the survey that's located in the appendix of this book, and we can be confident that we measured all six of their TRAITS accurately. Once again, we found that men were more likely to use PCs, and that the higher your meToo score, the more likely you were to prefer Macs. Information again didn't matter, which matches our Amazon results. One other trait, however, was important: Risk. People with higher risk acceptance were more likely to use a Mac, and the effect was almost as salient as the meToo attribute.

Despite the best efforts of Microsoft to be cool—including hiring Jerry Seinfeld for a recent campaign—it has not been easy. Macs and PCs have different sorts of users, and based on the Information and Time TRAITS, they're not separating based on the technical specifications of the hardware or concerns about the cost of the computer (which should have been picked up by the Time attribute). What is obvious, though, is that knowing the TRAITS of the people in your market is essential. As with our Google AdWords experiment, people filter the ads they're seeing in part based on their TRAITS. One way to sell your product supported by our research is to measure the TRAITS of potential customers and choose your ad campaign accordingly. If you're going after the fun-loving set that's driven by outward appearances, you should first make sure they exist in your market, and then design attractive computers for them.

WHAT'S LOVE GOT TO DO WITH IT?

A girl can tuck a Trojan into her purse on a Saturday night, but there is no such device to protect her heart.
—Laura Sessions Stepp, author of *Unhooked: How Young Women Pursue Sex, Delay Love, and Lose at Both*

In addition to its academics and sports programs, Duke is also noted for its party scene. Laura Sessions Stepp, a Pulitzer-winning journalist at the *Washington Post*, used Duke as a case study for her exposé on modern dating. Or, to be more accurate, the almost complete lack of dating. Her argument, which has a ring of truth to it according to the undergraduates we've talked to, is that in high school, kids are too busy to date. Unlike our generation, which didn't by and large do a lot of homework or participate in many extracurricular activities, getting into an elite college takes a lot of time these days. Every year we ask our students the average amount of time they spent after school doing homework or activities related to getting into college, and the most common answer is somewhere around five hours. Daily. Add that to the normal school hours, and you can see why college-bound high school students don't date.

In college, there's a lot more time, and as we've seen, some undergraduates use this time to win hundreds of thousands of dollars at poker. But they still don't date, according to Stepp.

Instead, the "hookup culture," as it has come to be known, has taken the place of dating. Instead of going through the world in pairs, many students are part of groups, and they don't want the commitment of even a short-term relationship.

Like every latest malady of youth culture that hits the news, the hookup culture has been the subject of less scholarly and more salacious journalism. Again, though, Duke has been the focus. *Rolling Stone* magazine, for one, has written about parties and hooking up in an article entitled "Sex and Scandal at Duke"—this article, like many others, was predicated by the media frenzy surrounding the lacrosse rape prosecution that occurred in 2006. We even have relatively highbrow (and salacious) fiction covering our campus excesses: Tom Wolfe wrote *I Am Charlotte Simmons* allegedly using Duke as a model.

Our last set of results takes aim at dating and marriage. Instead of using the TRAITS to win at poker, or win in the marketplace, we're going to look at how TRAITS influence the pursuit of love. Like the other choices we've explored in this chapter, we asked our undergraduates what they thought about two key topics: Would you ever consider using an online dating service? And do you think divorce is a good idea if couples have had extended problems?

Using Duke undergrads to look at this issue is interesting, since their personal lives have been the subject of numerous journalists. Yet we also have to preface these results with a warning. Usually we're sanguine about samples of undergrads—after all, we believe our TRAITS model is universal, and we have data from Amazon, Google, and Knowledge Networks to support this claim. But in the case of dating, Duke students might be idiosyncratic. They're not married. And if the journalists are right, and you're older than thirty, or you don't have a fancy college pedigree, our results may not apply to you.

When you look at these issues, demographics plus microtargeting aren't very helpful in explaining attitudes toward divorce and dating. Three of our TRAITS, however, do help explain these choices. High Information and Altruism scores indicate you're more likely to approve of divorce or try online dating. The role of Information is straightforward, especially for online dating; like any new technology, people who like Information will be the first to embrace it (and probably see it as an efficient way to meet people). Altruism is harder to pin down, but we suspect the effect comes down to trust. If you volunteer and care about the utility of others, you probably expect the favor will be returned and are more likely to use an online dating service. Our data don't include the history of success and failure with online dating, and it would be interesting to see how Information and Altruism interact with experience.

The meToo attribute, however, has a split role. A high meToo score indicates that you are less likely to use an online dating service. In all likelihood, this is because if you're highly other-regarding, you are meeting dates through your social networks and families and are more willing to look for dates in person. What's more curious is that a high meToo score means you're more approving of divorce. We'd bet that a couple of decades ago this effect would have been reversed; currently, though, Gallup reports that over 70 percent of Americans approve of divorce, and over half approve of living together (and many think that doing so reduces the chance of a future divorce). It may also be that people who care about their social networks perceive a lower risk of being isolated by getting a divorce.

These results will mean different things to different people. If you work for an online dating service, you'll have to develop a strategy to make people with lower Information scores aware of your service and comfortable with this relatively new technology. If you're going to reach people with extensive social networks, you're also going to have to convince them that online dating offers improvements over going out to a bar or dating a friend of a friend.

If you use online dating services, our results may make you confident that they're a good use of time and money. The person you meet online is likely to be more altruistic than average, and if you also value information, you may find a match made in heaven.

A last note: We asked a number of other questions about romance ranging from blind dating to living together, and our TRAITS did well in explaining all of them. There was, however, one exception. When it comes to love at first sight, about half of our respondents believed in it and half didn't. Neither demographics plus microtargeting, nor party identification, nor even our TRAITS explained who believed in this phenomenon. There are some things beyond the reach of science.

Conclusion

How do you find the people who might be interested
in your product, who simply need a nudge or a piece of additional information to go from browser to buyer? That's the daily dilemma of marketing. When the feminist fund-raising group Emily's List faced this quandary in the Iowa Democratic presidential caucus in 2008, the group got creative in microtargeting voters.

The political strategists at Emily's List set out to find women in Iowa who supported Hillary Clinton but were put off by the caucus process. The group already planned to buy search ads that popped up when people in Iowa entered political terms like "2008 caucus," "women for Hillary," "Social Security," or "global warming." But Emily's List also wanted to reach Hillary supporters who might not be thinking about the caucus process. So they started buying keywords not normally associated with politics, instead targeting terms like "recipe," "post-Thanksgiving sale," or "stocking stuffer." As Romano Oliver, the communications director of Emily's List, explained, "We really were trying to get women where they live." The result—over twenty thousand people across 613 Iowa towns clicked on the advertisement.

Though Emily's List is a feminist organization, they used the following logic to target their messages: Females are most likely to be Hillary Clinton supporters in Iowa; females are more likely to do online searches about cooking and shopping; therefore, we'll buy search terms like "recipe" and "toys." Both campaigns and companies engage in this type of microtargeting. Advertising messages are shaped and delivered based on a person's demographics (i.e., gender, age, and income) or lifestyle (i.e., church attendance, gun ownership, TV viewership).

This microtargeting strategy can miss important differences among women searching for recipes on the Internet. Some will want political appeals with lots of information, and others will be more interested in what friends and family are choosing. As we saw in the previous chapter, some of those who are searching the Web for safety products such as a lead test will click on a political ad that mentions risk too.

Marketers today crunch large amounts of data in search of lifestyle and product associations and correlations. Yet in sifting through the millions of decisions each of us makes each year, what companies often miss is the observation that people vary systemically in *how* they make decisions. On the surface, decisions about driving, eating, investing, and voting look very different. Yet the TRAITS model shows that these decisions share many common elements, so that a given person will approach each of them in the same way.

In making a choice, you face decisions about whether to revise what you've done before, gather more information, or look to the decisions of others. You consider how much you value distant payoffs, how much you fear negative outcomes, how much you care about the needs of other people. The good news for us as researchers, and for you as a reader, is that a particular person reaches decisions in similar ways across many different areas of life. This means that choices about products and people and politics can be combined systematically and used to predict what a person will buy or do or believe. Our results consistently show that adding TRAITS to other models of choice allows you to predict more accurately how a person behaves as a consumer, neighbor, and voter.

WHAT IS TO BE DONE?

The question now becomes, how can you use TRAITS to predict the choices you care about? There are four strategic ways you can use TRAITS: Algorithm, Cluster, Similarity, and Introspection.

Data on the decisions you make each day are collected and circulated widely. Consumer research firms such as ChoicePoint and Acxiom sell information about your purchasing habits. Web sites track your visits, building a profile of your reading interests. Google and Yahoo! track your searches. You may choose to share your beliefs and preferences through reviews on Amazon, status updates on Facebook, or posts on blogs and Twitter, all of which provide even more data for companies to mine. Even your civic life, captured through your voter registration information and voting frequency, is recorded in databases maintained by the Democratic and Republican national committees, and by commercial firms specializing in political data such as Aristotle and Catalist.

If you work for a firm that already buys consumer information, you can use the Algorithm strategy. With lots of consumer data, you can develop statistical models (i.e., algorithms) to predict choices. TRAITS can tell you what decisions to track and how to separate your data into the salient types of people (as defined by their styles of decision making, or TRAITS). Think hard about the dimensions of your product. Does it involve benefits that occur today (like the pleasures of eating ice cream), or far in the future (such as the payouts from a retirement fund)? Is it risky? Will it have positive spillovers on others, such as a Fair Trade product? Does understanding its operation involve a lot of information, like knowing how to use the options on a computer? Will it appeal to people who worry about the perceptions of others? Has the brand inspired loyalty in consumers, or are you entering the market with a very new product? The answers to these questions will tell you how important modeling particular TRAITS will be in predicting who might use your product.

By buying information on individual consumers, you can develop models that predict how likely they will be to use your product. This allows you to target particular segments of consumers for more information and persuasion. The results from our Google tests suggest that TRAITS can also help you frame your approach. For consumers who hate risk, you can praise a product's safety. For those scoring high on meToo, you can stress how widely used and recognized a product is.

The wide availability of data on individuals' decisions means that, for many companies, it will be feasible to use the Algorithm strategy to model consumer behavior. But there are shortcuts for guessing which people are likely to buy your products or consume your ideas. We dub one such strategy Cluster, since it relies on the observation that particular configurations of TRAITS come in clusters. Theoretically, people can be either high or low on each of the six TRAITS, giving us sixty-four distinct approaches to decision making. Yet when we examined the Knowledge Networks data, we found that, in general, there were four types of decision makers, each with its own unique cluster of TRAITS. We call these decision archetypes the Gambler, the Fan, the Shopper, and the Drifter.

The Gambler sticks with his decisions, loves risk, focuses on today, and is low on Altruism and information seeking. The Fan is loyal and risk seeking too. But he also loves information, is high on Altruism, looks to the decisions of others, and thinks about the future. The Shopper is more pragmatic, gathering information, looking to the choices of others, focusing on today, and remaining flexible about changing decisions. The Drifter, in contrast, barely registers connections. He's low on Altruism, Information, meToo, and Stickiness, and is very willing to take risks. Though three out of the four most frequent clusters are high on Risk, many other configurations that occur with less frequency involve people who are much happier avoiding risks.

While you may not have detailed TRAITS data on individuals, you may have enough information about your customers (Are they loyal? Involved in the community? Consumers of information?) to extrapolate their clusters. This will allow you to target them with specific products and to frame arguments for your advertising. If you were targeting car advertisements based on the TRAITS clusters, for example, the text you used to reach particular clusters would vary.

To reach Fans, you might talk in terms of altruism—saving the environment, protecting U.S. automaking jobs, or making sure that the kids in the backseat are okay. For the Shopper, you'd provide lots of information about product details and stress how many others were using the car and were happy with it. For the Gambler, you'd talk about brands (since they're high on Stickiness) and the immediate benefits of driving this particular car today. You might not have much luck with using particular arguments to reach the Drifter, though the TRAITS suggest which frames might not work. He's not altruistic, doesn't gather information or look to others, and is very willing to change his mind. You might be better off experimenting with variables like pricing to see what the Drifter responds to.

The Similarity strategy builds on the insight that a person's TRAITS affect his choices across different areas of decision making. It earns its name because one way to target consumers is to think about a decision from another area of life that is similar to the one you're trying to influence. Imagine you were set to introduce a high-tech product targeted at people in their thirties. Chapter 6 shows that early adopters of new products share a common set of TRAITS. They are more likely to take risks and enjoy consuming information. They're also much less likely to look to the decisions of others for status or acceptance and much less likely to stick with previous decisions.

If you add in a dose of altruism, as we saw earlier, this same combination of TRAITS predicts people who choose to be political independents. People who reject a party label and report that they are independents are, controlling for demographic factors like age and education, more likely to accept risks, gather information, revisit their decisions, and not simply follow the decisions of others. Buying a list of people who register as political independents in a state is an easy shortcut to finding potential consumers to target as early adopters.

Data from politics can help you find customers too if your product involves consumption of an idea or identity. Some products involve making a choice to change the world. This includes goods that generate less pollution, like hybrid cars, or that are made by employees earning living wages under equitable working conditions. These products often carry a higher price, but some people are willing to pay a premium to express their support or confirm their identity as a moral consumer. The impact of a single consumer's actions is tiny. Yet the growth of green marketing, Fair Trade commodities, and anti-sweatshop goods show that some consumers are willing to pay a price for identity consumption.

How can you find people who are fans of ideas or identities? One source is voter registration records. People who register and vote frequently are like people who buy Fair Trade coffee or environmentally friendly products. They're willing to bear a cost, in this case taking the time to vote, to make a statement and contribute to a collective decision. As one person among thousands or millions in your community, if you don't show up to vote the outcome of the election won't change. If you fail to buy the energy-saving lightbulb because it is more expensive up front, your extra energy consumption won't cause an additional power plant to be built. But there are a set of people who do take small actions that in aggregate end up benefiting society, in part because they like expressing their beliefs and consuming an identity. And if you want to find them as consumers, a place to start is by looking for them as voters.

Using Algorithm, Cluster, and Similarity strategies, you can harness TRAITS to target customers and frame your message for particular audiences. But we also promised in the introduction that TRAITS can help move an audience of one—you. Now that you've seen how the TRAITS work, go back to the results from the test you took in the appendix. If you failed to take the test while reading chapter 1, that might indicate you place a low value on the future and on information. (To confirm that, try taking the test after you read this paragraph if you haven't already.)

With the results of your own TRAITS test in hand, it may be time for Introspection. We don't believe that a particular set of TRAITS is good or bad. But the dangers of being at the extremes of any given spectrum are clear. If you're totally focused on outcomes today, you will miss out on opportunities in the future. Likewise, if you're always thinking about tomorrow, you may miss what today has to offer. In chapter 3 we saw that some TRAITS lead people to report more happiness with their decisions. Those who thought about the future, sought out information, and were altruistic reported more satisfaction with many aspects of their lives, including their houses, neighborhoods, and standards of living. People who were high on risk-taking, on the other hand, were less satisfied with their material possessions and the quality of their lives.

If you take the TRAITS test and discover that you place a low value on the future, are less interested in information, like to take risks, and are loyal to past decisions, you may want to target your own decisions for change.

You should recognize that this combination of TRAITS, which we call the Gambler, means that you're less likely to get what you're after when you make decisions. To combat this problem, you may want to set aside more time to gather information, take a longer-range view when you're making decisions, and consider the possible downsides to the options that you face. You may not be able to alter your TRAITS, but once you recognize their implications you can take steps to counteract their effects if you don't like where they're leading you.

Appendix:
What Are Your TRAITS?

INSTRUCTIONS: For each trait, answer the five questions and tally up your score. Do not leave any question blank. When you are done, you'll have a positive or a negative score for each trait. For example, if you have a positive score for the Time trait, you look toward the future; a negative score indicates you are focused on today.

Do you floss your teeth daily?

    +1 yes   −1 no

Do you exercise two or more times per week?

    +1 yes   −1 no

Do you eat healthy food most of the time?

    +1 yes   −1 no

Do you always lock your door no matter how long you'll be gone?

    +1 yes   −1 no

Do you prefer to buy the most extensive or the minimal necessary insurance?

    +1 extensive   −1 minimal

─────────────── *ADD UP YOUR ANSWERS HERE:* ───────────────

TIME:

−5	−4	−3	−2	−1	+1	+2	+3	+4	+5

[ignore the future]   [value the future]

Do yellow lights mean speed up or slow down?

+1 speed up   −1 slow down

Do you sometimes drink until intoxication?

+1 yes   −1 no

Do you enjoy gambling or making bets?

+1 yes   −1 no

Do you like roller coasters and other scary rides?

+1 yes   −1 no

How many speeding tickets have you had in the last five years?

+1 two or more   −1 one or fewer

─────────────── *ADD UP YOUR ANSWERS HERE:* ───────────────

RISK:

−5	−4	−3	−2	−1	+1	+2	+3	+4	+5

[averse]   [acceptant]

Do you believe people should report a crime if they see one?

+1 yes   −1 no

Should people feel compelled to serve on juries?

+1 yes   −1 no

Do you donate blood regularly?

+1 yes   −1 no

Do you recycle regularly or only when it is convenient?

+1 regularly   −1 when convenient

Do you think it is important to give to charities?

+1 yes   −1 no

--- ADD UP YOUR ANSWERS HERE: ---

ALTRUISM:

−5	−4	−3	−2	−1	+1	+2	+3	+4	+5
[self-concerned]								[other-concerned]	

Do you often read more than two books for pleasure in a month?

+1 yes   −1 no

Do you watch *The Daily Show* or *The Colbert Report*?

+1 yes   −1 no

Do you like to read reviews before going to a movie or making a purchase?

+1 yes   −1 no

Do you read the news on the Internet daily or subscribe to a newspaper/newsmagazine?

+1 yes   −1 no

Do you like to try different flavors of ice cream before choosing one?

+1 yes   −1 no

--- ADD UP YOUR ANSWERS HERE: ---

INFORMATION:

−5	−4	−3	−2	−1	+1	+2	+3	+4	+5
[info costly]								[info geek]	

Do you socialize with your neighbors?

+1 yes   −1 no

Do you frequently call your friends and family on the phone just to talk?

+1 yes   −1 no

Is dressing well important to success?

+1 yes   −1 no

Are people impressed by a great car or a well-furnished house?

+1 yes   −1 no

Should each homeowner be allowed to do whatever they like with their property or are covenants necessary to maintain the quality of the neighborhood?

+1 covenant needed   −1 no covenant

--------------------- ADD UP YOUR ANSWERS HERE: ---------------------

METOO:

−5	−4	−3	−2	−1	+1	+2	+3	+4	+5
[individualistic]							[other-regarding]		

Are you a consistent fan of any major league sports team?

+1 yes   −1 no

Do you like to try new restaurants or would you rather stick with a favorite?

+1 favorite   −1 new

Do you have favorite articles of clothing or do you just wear whatever is handy?

+1 favorite   −1 whatever

Would you rather buy American products when possible?

    +1 yes   −1 it doesn't matter

Do you enjoy foreign travel?

    +1 no   −1 yes

ADD UP YOUR ANSWERS HERE:

STICKINESS:

−5	−4	−3	−2	−1	+1	+2	+3	+4	+5

[independent]   [loyal]

References

INTRODUCTION

In some collections of numbers, if you pull off the numbers' first digits and look at their distribution you'll see a decreasing distribution (i.e., 1s are more frequent than 2s as first digits, which are more frequent than 3s). This phenomenon is called Benford's law. When people fudge their numbers, they fail to lie in a manner that replicates this distribution. We used this insight to compare monitored concentrations of chemicals with the self-reported pollution data that firms were reporting to the EPA. Our analysis showed that for two regulated chemicals, lead and nitric acid, firms were not accurately reporting their air emissions. See Scott de Marchi and James T. Hamilton, "Assessing the Accuracy of Self-reported Data: An Evaluation of the Toxics Release Inventory," *Journal of Risk and Uncertainty* 32, no. 1 (January 2006): 57–76.

The data and descriptions of high school dating come from Peter S. Bearman, James Moody, and Katherine Stovel, "Chains of Affection: The Structure of Adolescent Romantic and Sexual Networks," *American Journal of Sociology* 110, no. 1 (July 2004): 44–91.

1   HOW YOU DECIDE

Debates about how people choose often break down into "schools of thought." The rational-choice approach is often identified with the work of Gary Becker; see Gary Becker, "Nobel Lecture: The Economic Way of Looking at Behavior," *Journal of Political Economy* 101, no. 3 (1993): 385–409, and George J. Stigler and Gary S. Becker, "De Gustibus Non Disputandum," *American Economic Review* 67, no. 2 (March 1977): 76–90. Becker even applied the model to develop a theory of rational addiction, which he applied to the case of cigarette addiction. See Gary S. Becker and Kevin M. Murphy, "A Theory of Rational Addiction," *Journal of Political Economy* 96, no. 4 (August 1988): 675–700, and Gary S. Becker, Michael Grossman, and Kevin M. Murphy, "An Empirical Analysis of Cigarette Addiction," *American Economic Review* 84, no. 3 (June 1994): 396–418. The core rational model emphasizes how choices respond to changes in incentives (e.g., prices) and constraints. Highly effective accounts of decision-making that stress the impact of incentives on choice include Steven D. Levitt and Stephen J. Dubner, *Freakonomics: A Rogue Economist Explores the Hidden Side of Everything* (New York: William Morrow, 2005), and Tyler Cowen's *Discover Your Inner Economist: Use Incentives to Fall in Love, Survive Your Next Meeting, and Motivate Your Dentist* (New York: Dutton, 2007).

A second stream of research emphasizes how imperfections in human decision-making and the importance of the framing or context of a choice can influence the desirability of the choices made. An increasingly popular part of this research is the field of behavioral economics. Two excellent introductions to the importance of understanding behavioral anomalies are Dan Ariely's *Predictably Irrational: The Hidden Forces That Shape Our Decisions* (New York: HarperCollins, 2008), and Richard H. Thaler and Cass R. Sunstein, *Nudge: Improving Decisions About Health, Wealth, and Happiness* (New Haven: Yale University Press, 2008). See also Daniel Kahneman's "Maps of Bounded Rationality: Psychology for Behavioral Economics," *American Economic Review* 93, no. 5 (December 2003): 1449–75.

Scholars have identified shortcuts, or heuristics, people use in decision-making that can help them economize on what they need to know to make the proper choice, given their preferences. Samuel Popkin shows in *The Reasoning Voter: Communication and Persuasion in Presidential Campaigns* (Chicago: University of Chicago Press, 1991) how voters can choose candidates effectively using "low-information rationality," which may involve rules of thumb and shortcuts that allow them to make judgments about politicians without gathering large amounts of data. For a general theory of heuristics, see Daniel Kahneman and Shane Frederick, "A Model of Heuristic Judgment," in *Cambridge Handbook of Thinking and Reasoning*, edited by Keith J. Holyoak and Robert G. Morrison (Cambridge, UK: Cambridge University Press, 2005).

A famous paradox in rational choice theory that is in part analogous to our example of the economist crossing the road is the St. Petersburg Paradox; see Paul Samuelson's "St. Petersburg Paradoxes: Defanged, Dissected, and Historically Described," *Journal of Economic Literature* (1977).

To follow Herbert Simon's ant on the beach, see Herbert A. Simon, *The Sciences of the Artificial*, 3rd ed. (Cambridge, MA: MIT Press, 1996). Other scholars have followed Simon in asserting the importance of bounded rationality and diversity in explaining human behavior. Scott Page's book *The Difference: How the Power of Diversity Creates Better Groups, Firms, Schools, and Societies* (Princeton, NJ: Princeton University Press, 2008) shows how organizations with heterogeneity arrive at better decisions than do those that are more homogeneous. In political science, researchers have shown that political parties, members of Congress, and voters are in fact very diverse and employ different approaches to decision making; two good examples of this literature are Ken Kollman, John Miller, and Scott Page, "Adaptive Parties in Spatial Elections," *American Political Science Review* 86 (1992): 929–37; and Michael Laver, "Policy and the Dynamics of Political Competition," *American Political Science Review* 99 (2005) 263–81.

For more details on Danny Glover's 1999 complaint with the New York City Taxi and Limousine Commission that a cab driver discriminated against him and the 2009 experiment by *Good Morning America* that looked at whether race played a role in cab driver decisions about whom to stop for at night, see "Danny Glover Says Cabbies Discriminated Against Him" by Monte Williams, *New York Times*, November 4, 1999; "New York City to Pay Settlement to Taxi Drivers Accused of Bias" by Thomas J. Lueck, *New York Times*, March 8, 2006; and "Race for a Cab: When Hailing a Ride Isn't So Black and White" (November 4, 1999) at http://abcnews.go.com/GMA/story?id=7223511&page=1.

Tempting four-year-olds with marshmallows and cookies as a way to study the "ability to delay gratification" (ATDG) is a favored research method in psychology. See Desiree M. Seeyave, "Ability to Delay Gratification at Age 4 Years and Risk of Overweight at Age 11 Years," *Archives of Pediatrics and Adolescent Medicine* 163, no. 4 (April 2009): 303–8. Some children do exhibit a higher ATDG than others, just as some adults in our sample focus more on future outcomes than others who are more focused on current results. We do not attempt to determine the degree to which differences in TRAITS like the focus on today versus the future arise from nature versus nurture. We expect that they are likely from some combination of heredity, environment, and the interaction between these factors. In our work we simply take a snapshot of a person's TRAITS as his way of approaching decisions now, and predict choices based on that set of TRAITS. For a description of the original marshmallow studies at the Bing Nursery School at Stanford in the 1960s, see Jonah Lehrer, "Don't! The Secret of Self-Control," *New Yorker*, May 18, 2009.

For a discussion of fast food in America and ratings of chicken sandwiches, see "Fast Food: Adding Health to the Menu," *Consumer Reports* 69, no. 9 (September 2004). Michael Pollan's *The Omnivore's Dilemma: A Natural History of Four Meals* (New York: Penguin, 2006) describes the wiggle room in the term "free-range" chicken. Claudia Deutsch in "Advertising: Trying to Connect the Dinner Plate to Climate Change," *New York Times*, August 29, 2007, charts the attempt to link eating habits with concern for carbon footprints.

Economists are starting to study more often how people discount the future across different types of decisions. See Gretchen B. Chapman and Arthur S. Elstein, "Valuing the Future: Temporal Discounting of Health and Money," *Medical Decision Making* 15, no. 4 (October–December 1995): 373–86; Shane Frederick, George Loewenstein, and Ted O'Donoghue, "Time Discounting and Time Preference: A Critical Review," *Journal of Economic Literature*

40, no. 2 (June 2002): 351–401; and Jesse M. Shapiro's "Is There a Daily Discount Rate? Evidence from the Food Stamp Nutrition Cycle" (2003), working paper.

Joni Hersch and Kip Viscusi are leaders in the field of examining how smokers make decisions about other risks in their lives. See Joni Hersch, "Smoking, Seat Belts, and Other Risky Consumer Decisions: Differences by Gender and Race," *Managerial and Decision Economics* 17, no. 5 (September–October 1996): 471–81; Joni Hersch and W. Kip Viscusi, "Cigarette Smoking, Seatbelt Use, and Differences in Wage-Risk Tradeoffs," *Journal of Human Resources* 25, no. 2 (Spring 1990): 202–27; and W. Kip Viscusi's *Smoking: Making the Risky Decision* (New York: Oxford University Press, 1992). Other researchers looking at how preferences for risk may vary across decisions about health and wealth include Robert Barsky et al., "Preference Parameters and Behavioral Heterogeneity: An Experimental Approach in the Health and Retirement Study," *Quarterly Journal of Economics* 112, no. 2 (May 1997): 537–79; Alma Cohen and Liran Einav, "Estimating Risk Preferences from Deductible Choice," *American Economic Review* 97, no. 3 (June 2007): 745–88; David Cutler and Edward Glaeser, "What Explains Differences in Smoking, Drinking and Other Health-Related Behaviors" (February 2005), working paper; Jonathan Gruber, "Risky Behavior Among Youths: An Economic Analysis" (July 2000), working paper; Ted O'Donoghue and Matthew Rabin, "Risky Behavior Among Youths: Some Issues from Behavioral Economics" (2000), working paper E00'285; Matthew Rabin and Richard H. Thaler, "Anomalies: Risk Aversion," *Journal of Economic Perspectives* 15, no. 1 (Winter 2001): 219–32; and Marvin Zuckerman and D. Michael Kuhlman, "Personality and Risk-Taking: Common Biosocial Factors," *Journal of Personality* 68, no. 6 (December 2000): 999–1029.

Reactions to chemical attack scenarios are contained in Dru Sefton's "We'd Rather Die than Take Our Clothes Off, Disaster Planners Say," *Seattle Times*, May 25, 2002. FEMA's "After a Chemical Attack" advice on how to deal with contamination can be found at www.fema.gov.

Data on who gets the flu and the flu shot are found at the CDC's "Key Facts about Seasonal Influenza (Flu)," at http://www.cdc.gov/flu/keyfacts.htm, and Health Care Poll's "A Third of Public Has Had Flu Shots: Substantial Numbers Have Tried and Failed to Get Flu Shots for Children (12%) or Themselves (5%)," *Health Care Poll* 2, no. 14 (December 30, 2003). Research predicting who chooses to get the flu shot includes Gretchen B. Chapman and Elliot J. Coups, "Time Preferences and Preventive Health Behavior: Acceptance of the Influenza Vaccine," *Medical Decision Making* 19 (1999): 307–14, and John Mullahy's "It'll Only Hurt a Second? Microeconomic Determinants of Who Gets Flu Shots," *Health and Economics* 8 (1999): 9–24.

The card-counting skills of a band of MIT students who reaped great profits at casinos in the 1990s are recounted in the books Ben Mezrich's books *Bringing Down the House: The Inside Story of Six MIT Students Who Took Vegas for Millions* (New York: Free Press, 2002) and *Busting Vegas: The MIT Whiz Kid Who Brought the Casinos to Their Knees* (New York: HarperCollins, 2005) and in the films *21* and *Breaking Vegas*.

Our graphs convey results from multiple regression analyses that use the Knowledge Networks data to predict many different choices made by the approximately thirty thousand respondents in our sample. For more technical information on how we conducted these statistical analyses, see www.youchoosebook.com.

2 YOU ARE WHAT YOU CHOOSE

For the announcement of Tuna Amobi's award, see *Wall Street Journal Online*, "Best on the Street 2008," May 21, 2008. Research on whether there are actually long-term differences in the recommendations of analysts can be found in Michael B. Mikhail, Beverly R. Walther, and Richard H. Willis, "Do Security Analysts Exhibit Persistent Differences in Stock Picking Ability?" *Journal of Financial Economics* 74 (2004): 67–91. In "Are the Wall Street Analyst Rankings Popularity Contests?" (2007), Douglas Emery and Xi Li found that in the year after winning the Best on the Street award, these star analysts "perform significantly worse" than the nonstar analysts.

Discussions of the bias toward publishing "positive results" in medical research include Jason T. Connor, "Positive Reasons for Publishing Negative Findings," *American Journal of Gastroenterology* 103 (2008): 2181–83; Anton K. Forman, "Estimating the Proportion of Studies Missing for Meta-analysis Due to Publication Bias," *Contemporary Clinical Trials* 29 (2008): 732–39; and Katie Dunn, "Selective Publication and Its Impact on Clinical Knowledge," *Journal of Small Animal Practice* 50 (January 2009): 1–2.

Microtargeting usually refers to a strategy of using large amounts of data about people's lifestyle decisions to predict their consumer and political choices. Recent descriptions of how algorithms and data can sort people into groups to target with ads or other information include Ian Ayres's *Super Crunchers: Why Thinking-by-Numbers Is the New Way to Be Smart* (New York: Bantam, 2007); Stephen Baker's *The Numerati* (Boston: Houghton Mifflin Harcourt, 2008); Bill Bishop's *The Big Sort: Why the Clustering of Like-Minded America Is Tearing Us Apart* (Boston: Houghton Mifflin, 2008); and Mark J. Penn's *Microtrends: The Small Forces Behind Tomorrow's Big Changes* (New York: Twelve, 2007).

Tales of speeding in the United States are found in David Shaftel, "Tale of Outlaw Racing, with the U.S. as a Course," *New York Times*, October 17, 2007, while Finnish speeding is discussed by BBC News in "Nokia Boss Gets Record Speeding Fine" from January 14, 2002, available at http://news.bbc .co.uk/2/hi/europe/1759791.stm. Research using Finnish driving records, tax filings, and psychological profiles from armed forces tests is presented in Mark

Grinblatt and Matti Keloharju, "Sensation Seeking, Overconfidence, and Trading Activity" (May 2006), NBER Working Paper 12223. More on Finns and driving from BBC News in "Finn's Speed Fine Is a Bit Rich" from February 10, 2004, available at http://news.bbc.co.uk/1/hi/business/3477285.stm. For a very diverting first-person account of the need for speed, see Alexander Roy's *The Driver: My Dangerous Pursuit of Speed and Truth in the Outlaw Racing World* (New York: HarperEntertainment, 2007).

The impact of gay marriage on voting in the 2004 presidential election attracted the immediate attention of journalists (see "Was Same-Sex Marriage Partly to Blame for Kerry Loss?," November 5, 2004, at http://abcnews.go.com/WNT/story?id=230634&page=1; and "Gay Marriage: Did Issue Help Re-Elect Bush?" from *SFGate.com*, November 4, 2004, at http://www.sfgate.com/cgi-bin/article.cgi?f=/c/a/2004/11/04/MNG3A9LLVI1.DTL) and long-term interest by academics (see Gregory B. Lewis, "Same-sex Marriage and the 2004 Presidential Election," April 2005, *PSOnline*, at http://www.apsanet.org/imgtest/PSApr05Lewis.pdf; and David E. Campbell and J. Quin Monson, "The Religion Card: Gay Marriage and the 2004 Presidential Election," *Public Opinion Quarterly* 72, no. 3 [Fall 2008]: 399–419).

Memorable Howard Dean quotes are in Jill Lawrence's "Pre-Prime-Time Dean Takes Sharper Tone," *USA Today*, July 27, 2004, available at http://www.usatoday.com/news/politicselections/nation/president/2004-07-27-dean-usat_x.htm.

The Commission on Presidential Debates provides full transcripts of presidential debates, including the 2004 vice presidential debate, at www.debates.org.

In his coauthored book about social issues and politics, Morris Fiorina has a chapter entitled "A Closer Look at Homosexuality" in which he details how views on this issue have shifted over time within political parties in the United States. See *Culture War? The Myth of a Polarized America* (New York: Pearson Longman, 2005). Doctors, biochemists, and economists all have distinct ways of viewing the health effects of alcohol. See Joseph A. Baur et al., "Resveratrol Improves Health and Survival of Mice on a High-Calorie Diet," *Nature* 444 (November 16, 2006): 337–42; Philip J. Cook, *Paying the Tab: The Costs and Benefits of Alcohol Control* (Princeton, NJ: Princeton University Press, 2007); and Cecil R. Pace-Asciak et al., "The Red Wine Phenolics *Trans*-Resveratrol and Quercetin Block Human Platelet Aggregation and Eicosanoid Synthesis: Implications for Protection Against Coronary Heart Disease," *Clinica Chimica Acta* 235 (1995): 207–19.

3   HAPPY, HEALTHY, AND WISE

A short history of lawn chair flight is provided by Thomas Vinciguerra in "Grab Your Lawn Chair. Float Away," *New York Times*, July 13, 2008. The sport is attracting more attention than practitioners, with one analysis noting, "Cluster ballooning is still a fringe sport. There are fewer than a dozen people worldwide who have flown cluster balloons." See "Cluster Balloon Travel," available at http://www.greenmuze.com/climate/travel/946-cluster-ballooning .html. The story of Father de Carli is recounted in "Flying Priest's Survival Chances Fade," April 23, 2008, at http://www.msnbc.msn.com/id/24277336/.

Stories about Britney Spears's driving mishaps include Karen Thomas, "Can Britney Spears Bounce Back?" *USA Today*, October 10, 2007, at http://www .usatoday.com/life/people/2007-10-01-britney-spears_N.htm; "Britney Spears' Latest Parenting Mishap" (2006), at http://abcnews.go.com/GMA/Entertainment/ Story?id=1971687&page=1; "Britney Spears Gets Driver's License," *USA Today*, October 4, 2007, at http://www.usatoday.com/life/people/2007-10-03-spears_N .htm; "Judge Orders Britney Spears to Be Booked," *USA Today*, October 6, 2007; "Britney Spears Explains Her Lack of Car Seat" (February 7, 2006), at http://www .parentdish.com/2006/02/07/britney-spears-explains-her-lack-of-car-seat/; "Baby Seats: Don't Pull a Britney" (May 18, 2006), at http://blogs.consumerreports .org/cars/2006/05/baby_seats_dont.html; and "Britney Spears: Spotlight on Car-Seat Safety" (June 2006), at http://www.consumerreports.org/cro/ babies-kids/baby-toddler/travel-gear/car-seats/britney-spears-spotlight-on-car -seat-safety-6-06/overview/britney-spears-spotlight-on-car-seat-safety-6-06.htm.

Nicole Nason's work as head of the National Highway Traffic Safety Administration and her trouble installing a child car seat are detailed in "NHTSA Pledges Some Safety Actions by Year-End," *Detroit News*, September 20, 2007; Jane O'Donnell, "Diplomacy, Humor Take New NHTSA Chief Far," *USA Today*, September 25, 2006, at http://www.usatoday.com/educate/ reading/20070328_Nissan_Diplomacy.pdf; and Sara Lacey, "Even NHTSA Boss Can't Get Her Car Seats Right," at http://www.motherproof.com/news-rants/story/even-nhtsa-boss-cant-get-her-car-seats-right/.

Stanley Fish dissects academics and Volvos in "The Unbearable Ugliness of Volvos," in *There's No Such Thing as Free Speech . . . and It's a Good Thing, Too* (New York: Oxford University Press, 1994).

Survey data on how party identification varies by car brand are discussed in John Tierney, "Your Car: Politics on Wheels," *New York Times*, April 1, 2005.

To see a dramatic ad about car safety, go to www.youtube.com and type in "Volvo Twister."

Vacillating views of fiber are evident in publications such as Denis Parsons Burkitt, *Don't Forget Fibre in Your Diet* (London: Taylor and Francis, 1979); Judith A. Marlett et al., "Position of the American Dietetic Association: Health Implications of Dietary Fiber," *Journal of the American Dietetic Association* 102, no. 7 (July 2002): 993–1000; Charles S. Fuchs et al., "Dietary Fiber and the Risk of Colorectal Cancer and Adenoma in Women," *New England Journal of Medicine* 340, no. 3 (January 21, 1999): 169–76; and Joan Raymond, "Is Fiber the New Protein?" at http://www.newsweek.com/id/35662. The results of the 1999 study that found no connection between a high fiber diet and colorectal cancer in women are presented in "Dietary Fiber and the Risk of Colorectal Cancer and Adenoma in Women," *New England Journal of Medicine* 340, no. 3 (January 21, 1999): 169–76.

Jared's Subway ad story is told in Chip and Dan Heath's *Made to Stick: Why Some Ideas Survive and Others Die* (New York: Random House), 218–24.

Timothy Egan describes strong support in 2006 for President Bush in his article "All Polls Aside, Utah Is Keeping Faith in Bush," *New York Times*, June 4, 2006.

Detailed data on presidential approval ratings over time are available at www.ropercenter.uconn.edu.

The range of examples in this chapter show how our work differs from the approach often adopted by data mining firms, who take a given choice to predict and search for variables that are correlated with this decision. The set of variables selected will vary widely, and there is often no underlying story about why particular ones are chosen. In contrast, we believe that the TRAITS model describes the way a person approaches decisions in many different areas of life. We thus keep the same set of TRAITS variables to use in modeling how a person makes a decision, and show that we can successfully use this model to predict decisions that on the surface look very different: whether a person gets his desired level of safety in a car, chooses to eat healthy food, or approved of President Bush.

4 ALL-CONSUMING

John Keegan's classic description of the Battle of the Somme comes from his book *The First World War* (New York: Knopf, 1998). The two passages quoted are from pp. 149 and 243. Economists are starting to study what motivates group loyalty among soldiers on the battlefield. In studying a sample of Union Army infantry companies in the Civil War, Dora Costa and Matthew Kahn examine desertion, arrest, and AWOL as measures of "cowardice and heroism." They conclude that "individual and company socioeconomic and demographic characteristics, ideology, and morale were important predictors of group loyalty in the Union Army." See Dora L. Costa and Matthew E. Kahn, "Cowards and Heroes: Group Loyalty in the American Civil War," *Quarterly Journal of Economics* (May 2003): 519–48.

Tales of committed voters and activists in the 2004 presidential election include Adam Nagourney and Abby Goodnough, "The 2004 Campaign: Florida; Passion and Election Disputes on Rise in Florida as Vote Nears," *New York Times*, October 28, 2004, and Justin Walker, "Dennis Kucinich and the 'Peace Train,'" from Justin Walker's Campaign Diary, January 9, 2004, at http://www.dukenews .duke.edu/mmedia/features/campaigndiary/campaign_peacetrain.html.

Consumer Reports compares mileage across car models at its Web site, www.consumerreports.org. Stories about hybrids and gas mileage claims include John Gartner, "Hybrid Mileage Comes Up Short," May 11, 2004, at http://www.wired.com/cars/energy/news/2004/05/63413; Nicholas Rufford and Jason Dawe, "Toyota Prius Proves a Gas Guzzler in a Race with BMW 520d," March 16, 2008, at http://www.timesonline.co.uk/tol/driving/used_car_reviews/article3552994.ece; and Cheryl Jensen, "Your Mileage May Still Vary," *New York Times*, November 16, 2008.

Growing literatures in both economics and political science explore what leads people to be green in the marketplace or the voting booth. See David Popp, "Altruism and the Demand for Environmental Quality," *Land Economics* 77, no. 3 (August 2001): 339–349, and Deborah Lynn Guber, *The Grassroots of a Green Revolution: Polling America on the Environment* (Cambridge, MA: MIT Press, 2003). Related research analyzes what drives political consumerism in general (see Dietlind Stolle, Marc Hooghe, and Michele Micheletti, "Politics in the Supermarket: Political Consumerism as a Form of Political Participation," *International Political Science Review* 26, no. 3 [2005]: 245–269), and what drives contributions to collective good such as charity (see Craig Landry et al., "Toward an Understanding of the Economics of Charity: Evidence from a Field Experiment" [2005], NBER Working Paper 11611).

In our analysis of who recycles, we break down the meToo variable into two separate factors. We create one variable that measures how much you care about image and status, which draws upon questions dealing with the importance of brands in making you feel accepted, whether you look at the product choices of others for guidance, and the importance you attach to material possessions. The second component captures how important spending time with friends and family is to you and the degree to which you are part of social networks of neighbors or people who share your interests. People who rank high on the status/materialism component of meToo aren't driven to recycle. Those who enjoy being part of social networks are more likely to recycle, which may be because the people they're interacting with are recycling too.

The origins of the cable channel Planet Green are described in Brian Stelter, "A Network to Make an Environmental Point," *New York Times*, June 2, 2008.

5   CONSUMING POLITICS

For stories of party activists and undecided voters in 2008, see David Usborne, "Independent Voters Hold the Key to Swing Primary," *Independent* (UK), January 15, 2008, and Lisa Wangsness, "Humbug! Campaign Workers Toil Away," *Boston Globe*, December 25, 2007. On the runs of Ralph Nader and Ron Paul, see CNN.com, "Loyal Nader Fans Pack Madison Square Garden," October 14, 2000, and Michael Falcone, "Ron Paul Makes an Appeal for Third-Party Candidates," *New York Times*, September 9, 2008. Nader's view on the 2008 elections in June 2007 are summarized in Roger Simon, "Nader Ponders

Run, Calls Clinton Coward," June 21, 2007, at http://www.politico.com/news/stories/0607/4580.html. The article opened with the observation that "Ralph Nader says he is seriously considering running for president in 2008 because he foresees another Tweedledum-Tweedledee election that offers little real choice to voters." Nader eventually did run for president in 2008 as an independent candidate, and captured less than one percent of the votes cast.

Political scientists and economists have started to explore political actions as identity consumption, expressive functions, and "fandom." See George A. Akerlof and Rachel E. Kranton, "Economics and Identity," *Quarterly Journal of Economics* 115, no. 3 (August 2000): 715–53; Geoffrey Brennan and Alan Hamlin, "Expressive Voting and Electoral Equilibrium," *Public Choice* 95 (1998): 149–75; Geoffrey Brennan and Loren Lomasky, *Democracy and Decision: The Pure Theory of Electoral Preference* (Cambridge, UK: Cambridge University Press, 1993); Sanford Gordon, Catherine Hafer, and Dimitri Landa, "Consumption or Investment? Campaign Contributions and the Structure of Executive Compensation" (2005), working paper; and Donald Green, Bradley Palmquist, and Eric Schickler, *Partisan Hearts and Minds* (New Haven, CT: Yale University Press, 2002). Bryan Caplan explores in detail the motivations for turning out to vote in *The Myth of the Rational Voter: Why Democracies Choose Bad Policies* (Princeton, NJ: Princeton University Press, 2007). Thomas Frank describes the role that social issues play in politics in *What's the Matter with Kansas? How Conservatives Won the Heart of America* (New York: Metropolitan Books, 2004). See also the critique by Larry Bartels, "What's the Matter with *What's the Matter with Kansas?*" *Quarterly Journal of Political Science* 1, no. 2 (2006): 201–26.

A partial text of Mary Carey's interview on *The Colbert Report* is at "Mary Carey Does D.C.," Daniel Kurtzman's Political Humor Blog (June 16, 2005), at http://politicalhumor.about.com/b/2005/06/16/mary-carey-does-dc.htm.

Matthew Dowd discusses political brands in Thomas B. Edsall's *Building Red America: The New Conservative Coalition and the Drive for Permanent Power* (New York: Basic Books, 2006), 61.

On the role of patience and altruism in political turnout, see James H. Fowler, Altruism and Turnout," *Journal of Politics* 68, no. 3 (August 2006): 674–83, and James H. Fowler and Cindy D. Kam, "Patience as a Political Virtue: Delayed Gratification and Turnout," *Political Behavior* 28 (2006): 113–28.

Grover Norquist's quote equating Republicans voting for taxes as "rat heads in Coke bottles" comes in the discussion of branding in Benjamin R. Barber's *Consumed: How Markets Corrupt Children, Infantilize Adults, and Swallow Citizens Whole* (New York: W. W. Norton, 2007), 205.

Jay Leno's thoughts on the flu shot come from CNN transcripts available at http://www.studentnews.cnn.com/TRANSCRIPTS/0410/24/sun.02.html.

Analyses of primary coverage, how many remembered who won the Iowa caucuses the weekend after the event, and the ratings for prime-time shows can be found in David Carr, "With Shows Like These, Forget Reruns," *New York Times,* January 14, 2008; Pew survey, "Intense Iowa Coverage Leads Many to Say 'Too Much': Post-Iowa, Democratic Candidates Still Most Visible," at http://people-press.org/report/383/intense-iowa-coverage-leads-many-to-say-too-much; and TV by the Numbers, "Overnight Results for Thursday, January 10," at http://tvbythenumbers.com/2008/01/11/overnight-results-for-thursday-january-10/2357.

Gareth Groves found out the dangers of parking his Hummer in a liberal voting precinct in Washington, D.C. The damage done to his car is described in Allison Klein, "Hummer Owner Gets Angry Message: Vandals Batter D.C. Man's SUV, Slash Its Tires and Scratch In an Eco Note," *Washington Post*, July 18, 2007.

John Zaller works through the relationships among education, media use, and ideology in *The Nature and Origins of Mass Opinion* (Cambridge, UK: Cambridge University Press, 1991) and "Perversities in the Ideal of the Informed Citizenry," paper presented at "The Transformation of Civic Life," Middle Tennessee State University, Murfreesboro and Nashville, TN, November 12–13, 1999.

Life in D.C. came in for apparent criticism, and then a defense, in Ezra Klein's blog posts "Types of Cities," available at http://www.prospect.org/csnc/blogs/ezraklein_archive?month=09&year=2007&base_name=types_of_cities, and "Why I Shouldn't Write About Urban Policy at 2am," at http://www.prospect.org/csnc/blogs/ezraklein_archive?month=09&year=2007&base_name=why_i_shouldnt_write_about_urb.

We found congressional staffers contributing to candidates and political organizations by using www.opensecrets.org and searching the employers listed in the contributions records. We then went to www.fec.gov, which provides the addresses listed for contributors. Using an address matching program from Geolytics, we placed home addresses in census block groups and analyzed the demographic composition of the neighborhoods where staffers choose to live.

The Clintons' investment quandary is recounted in Patrick Healy, "To Avoid Conflicts, Clintons Liquidate Holdings," *New York Times*, June 15, 2007.

Legislators' investments in companies came from financial disclosure forms posted at www.opensecrets.org, while corporate social responsibility ratings came from the Calvert CSR Ratings posted at www.calvert.com.

6 EARLY ADOPTERS

Everett Rogers popularized the term "early adopter" in his classic *Diffusion of Innovations* (New York: Free Press, 1962), which classified people who adopted a new technology by how early in the diffusion process they took up the innovation. In order of adoption, he identified people as innovators, early adopters, early majority, late majority, and laggards.

Ed Begley Jr.'s green lifestyle is featured in Edward Lewine, "Hollywood Green," *New York Times*, May 20, 2007; Norma Meyer, "A Green Card," *San Diego Union-Tribune*, January 5, 2007; and at www.edbegley.com.

Sony's travails with the PlayStation 3 are discussed in Ben Silverman, "Sony Has Lost Over $3 Billion on the PS3," Yahoo! Games, June 26, 2008, available at http://videogames.yahoo.com/feature/sony-has-lost-over-3-billion-on-the-ps3/1223467; Don Reisinger, "Why Sony Needs to (But Can't) Drop the Price of the PS3," CNET Digital Home, December 30, 2008, available at http://news.cnet.com/why-sony-needs-to-but-cant-drop-the-price-of-the-ps3/; and Kentaro Hamada and Sachi Izumi, "Sony May Post $1.1 Billion Operating Loss," Reuters, January 13, 2009, at http://www.reuters.com/article/ousiv/idU STRE50B7LN20090113?pageNumber=1&virtualBrandChannel=0.

If you're wondering whether your friends have Amazon Wish Lists, you can go to www.amazon.com and at the Wish List page search by name or e-mail address (and you can add in city information too).

States vary in how easy they make it to access voter registration data, with North Carolina leading the nation in making its registration data accessible to the public. To learn how you can order the state's voter registration and history files for $25 from the North Carolina State Board of Elections, see http://www.sboe.state.nc.us/.

Articles about Twitter are now a subgenre within coverage of technology, social networks, and fads. For examples, see Andrew Lavallee, "Friends Swap Twitters, and Frustration," *Wall Street Journal*, March 16, 2007; Michelle Slatalla, "If You Can't Let Go, Twitter," *New York Times*, February 14, 2008; and Max Chafkin, "Kevin Rose of Digg: The Most Famous Man on the Internet," FOXBusiness.com, November 9, 2008 at http://www.foxbusiness.com/story/small-business/kevin-rose-digg-famous-man-internet/.

For blog posts about early adopters and Twitter, see "Social Media Early Adopters: Pioneers, Settlers, and Colonists," June 6, 2008, available at http://www.web-strategist.com/blog/2008/06/06/social-media-early-adopters-pioneers-settlers-and-colonists/, and "Importance of Being an Early Adopter," May 17, 2008, available at http://mashable.com/2008/05/17/early-adoption/. To see the actual "tweets" quoted here from Barack Obama, Kevin Rose, and Robert Scoble, go to www.twitter.com.

Keith Poole's listing of 3,320 legislators casting votes in the House and Senate from 1973 to 2002 lists Ron Paul as the most conservative legislator. See "Is John Kerry a Liberal?" October 13, 2004, available at http://voteview.ucsd .edu/is_john_kerry_a_liberal.htm, and "Estimating a Basic Space from a Set of Issue Scales," *American Journal of Political Science* 42 (July 1998): 954–93.

7   TRAITS IN THE WILD

Insights into Jason Strasser's poker life come from his "Off-Topic: Options Trading, You Might Like It," September 2, 2008, available at http://forum-server.twoplustwo.com/19/high-stakes-pl-nl/off-topic-options-trading-you-might-like-289600/; Bridget Booher, "Mathematics, Logic, and Lady Luck," *Duke Magazine* (May–June 2006); and Alun Bowden, "Mo Money, No Life," *Inside Poker*, September 2008, available at http://www.insidepokermag.co.uk/poker/features/7302/talking_point.html.

In our survey of Duke students we asked them to report their Myers-Briggs personality type. In predicting their poker choices and opinions about relationships, we found that the TRAITS model did a better job of predicting their selections than their self-reported Myers-Briggs type.

In 2007, Princeton University Press issued a sixtieth anniversary edition of John von Neumann and Oskar Morgenstern, *Theory of Games and Economic Behavior* (Princeton, NJ: Princeton University Press, 2007).

We created Google AdWords campaigns that compared how often people clicked on an ad when they saw a text such as "Barack Obama's Biography" or "Is Obama Too Risky?" Both of these ads had the same body: "Quotes. Interviews. Video. Find Out For Yourself." Each also linked to the Obama channel on www.youtube.com. The ads appeared on the side of search responses when people searched for "lead test" or "movie guide." Google also placed the ads next to Web content related to these search terms. The market for ads next to Google search results is described in Adam Liptak, "Competing for Clients, and Paying by the Click," *New York Times*, October 15, 2007.

For reviews of Mac and PC ads, see Seth Stevenson, "Mac Attack: Apple's Mean-Spirited New Ad Campaign," *Slate* (June 19, 2006), available at http://www.slate.com/id/2143810/, and Wilson Rothman, "Microsoft's 'I'm a PC' Ad Beats Seinfeld (But Not Hodgman)," Gizmodo.com, September 18, 2008, at http://gizmodo.com/5052051/microsofts-im-a-pc-ad-beats-seinfeld-but-not-hodgman.

The original 1984 Mac ad can be found at http://www.youtube.com/watch?v=OYecfV3ubP8&feature=related. Note that Macs now use the same Intel-based hardware as PCs, leading to such articles as Eric Lai, "Analysts: Mac Buyers Still Pay More than PC Buyers for Same Hardware 'Guts,'" available at http://www.computerworld.com/action/article.do?command=view ArticleBasic&articleId=9128968.

Laura Sessions Stepp writes about relations between the sexes at Duke in *Unhooked: How Young Women Pursue Sex, Delay Love, and Lose at Both* (New York: Riverhead, 2007). See Barbara Meltz, "The Strings Attached to Noncommital Sex," *Boston Globe*, March 10, 2007.

Tom Wolfe, whose daughter went to Duke, reportedly used part of what he observed at the university in writing *I Am Charlotte Simmons* (New York: Farrar, Straus & Giroux, 2004). The book became a favorite of George W. Bush (see Elisabeth Bumiller, "Bush's Official Reading List, and a Racy Omission," *New York Times*, February 7, 2005). Wolfe described the writing of the book to John Freeman in "Tom Wolfe Returns with a Novel That—He Swears—Isn't About Life at Duke University," *Independent Weekly* (NC), December 1, 2004, available at http://www.indyweek.com/gyrobase/Content?oid=oid%3A23209.

Gallup polls on views about marriage and divorce include Lynda Lyons, "The Future of Marriage: Part II" July 30, 2002, at http://www.gallup.com/poll/6499/Future-Marriage-Part.aspx; Lydia Saad, "Cultural Tolerance for Divorce Grows to 70%," May 19, 2008, at http://www.gallup.com/poll/107380/Cultural-Tolerance-Divorce-Grows-70.aspx; and Saad, "By Age 24, Marriage Wins Out," August 11, 2008, at http://www.gallup.com/poll/109402/Age-24-Marriage-Wins.aspx.

CONCLUSION

The online efforts by Emily's List to get out the vote in the 2008 Iowa caucus season are described by Peter Slevin and Jose Antonio Vargas in "Obama Tries New Tactics to Get Out Vote in Iowa," *Washington Post*, December 31, 2007, available at http://www.washingtonpost.com/wp-dyn/content/article/2007/12/30/AR2007123002795.html?nav=rss_politics, and at the group's Web site at http://www.emilyslist.org/news/releases/iowa_women_vote/.

David Brooks analyzes the humor in lifestyle sociology in *Bobos in Paradise: The New Upper Class and How They Got There* (New York: Touchstone, 2000). Joseph Turow in *Breaking Up America: Advertisers and the New Media World* (Chicago: University of Chicago Press, 1997) and Ron Fournier, Douglas B. Sosnik, and Matthew Dowd in *Applebee's America: How Successful Political, Business, and Religious Leaders Connect with the New American Community* (New York: Simon and Schuster, 2006) explain how finely companies can target their customers. Bill Tancer describes in detail in *Click: Unexpected Insights for Business and Life* (New York: Hyperion, 2008) how search and click data on the Internet can be used in marketing. In *How We Decide* (New York: Houghton Mifflin Harcourt, 2009), Jonah Lehrer draws on recent insights from neuroscience to describe how people make decisions. What these and other books on marketing and decision making do not explore, however, is how individuals vary systematically in the way they approach decisions across many aspects of their lives. For example, people who are willing to accept risks in products and revisit their purchase decisions are also more likely to do the same in politics, and therefore call themselves independents. A main contribution of the TRAITS model is to show how a person's decision-making habits stay the same across different types of choices. This means that data on how you make decisions as a neighbor and voter can be used to predict your life as a consumer.

Claire Cain Miller describes how the (maximum) 140-character messages sent via Twitter represent a new data source for companies to mine in "Finding Utility in the Jumble of Twittered Thoughts," *New York Times*, April 14, 2009, available at http://www.nytimes.com/2009/04/14/technology/internet/14twitter.html.

APPENDIX: WHAT ARE YOUR TRAITS?

Social science surveys rarely include detailed data on the decisions an individual makes across many domains in her life. Political scientists poll about politics and government, economists gather survey data on labor markets or consumer purchases, and sociologists explore the role that friends and family play in a person's life. We are indebted to a private polling firm, Knowledge Networks, for their willingness to sell us access to their data for a fee manageable with academic budgets. The firm maintains a nationally representative panel of individuals willing to answer a series of surveys over the Internet. Asking the questions over the Internet and spacing the surveys over time allows Knowledge Networks to develop very detailed profiles of their survey participants. We worked with a sample of nearly thirty thousand respondents who had completed surveys about their basic demographics, health, financial services use, auto ownership and use, alcohol consumption, restaurant preferences, opinions about public affairs, lifestyle/hobby/friendship questions, and values profiles. The data are proprietary, which means we cannot share the individual-level responses for the sample we worked with. If you want to learn more about the surveys and how to contact the firm about their panel data, see www.knowledgenetworks.com.

We used responses from many different Knowledge Networks surveys to build our measures of core TRAITS. You might not have the time or patience to fill out a survey with all these questions. So to develop quicker indicators of the TRAITS, we've written our own questions and sampled questions often asked in publicly available surveys. In this appendix we use five questions for each of the TRAITS to get a read on where you rank on each of these ways that people approach decision making.

Index